United States-Taiwan
Security Ties

United States–Taiwan Security Ties

From Cold War to Beyond Containment

Dennis Van Vranken Hickey

 PRAEGER

Westport, Connecticut
London

rary of Congress Cataloging-in-Publication Data

key, Dennis Van Vranken.
  United States-Taiwan security ties : from Cold War to beyond
ontainment / Dennis Van Vranken Hickey.
    p.   cm.
  Includes bibliographical references and index.
  ISBN 0-275-94672-X (alk. paper)
  1. United States—Foreign relations—Taiwan. 2. Taiwan—Foreign
:lations—United States. 3. United States—Military relations—
aiwan. 4. Taiwan—Military relations—United States.   I. Title.
183.8.T3H53 1994
27.73051249—dc20   93-1649

British Library Cataloguing in Publication Data is available.

Library of Congress Catalog Card Number: 93-1649
ISBN: 0-275-94672-X

First published in 1994

Praeger Publishers, 88 Post Road West, Westport, CT 06881
An imprint of Greenwood Publishing Group, Inc.

Printed in the United States of America

The paper used in this book complies with the
Permanent Paper Standard issued by the National
Information Standards Organization (Z39.48-1984).

10 9 8 7 6 5 4 3 2 1

Copyright Acknowledgments

The author and publisher gratefully acknowledge permission to reprint material from the
following copyrighted sources.

"American Technological Assistance, Technology Transfers and Taiwan's Drive for Self-
Sufficiency," by Dennis Van Vranken Hickey, in *The Journal of Northeast Asian Studies*
(Fall, 1989).

"China's Security Threat to Taiwan," by Dennis Van Vranken Hickey, in *Pacific Review*
(1992). Reprinted by permission of Oxford University Press.

To my wife, Cheng-May

Contents

Acknowledgments

This book would not have been possible without the support and encouragement of many special people. I thank Dr. James R. Roach and Dr. Gordon Bennett of the Department of Government at the University of Texas at Austin for their advice and encouragement during the initial stages of this project. Raymond Pai and Moses Lu of the Information Division at the Coordination Council for North American Affairs' branch office in Chicago provided resource materials and helped to arrange interviews with government officials in Taipei. I am grateful for their help. In addition, my gratitude goes to Byron Stewart and Tammy Stewart, the US government document librarians at Southwest Missouri State University's Duane Meyer Library. I especially appreciated their help in obtaining numerous government documents relevant to this study. Finally, I thank Southwest Missouri State University and the Pacific Cultural Foundation for their generous support. Over the past several years, both institutions provided me with assistance that helped me to complete this book.

   This study represents part of my continuing effort to examine the complicated web of security ties that exists between the United States and East Asia. An earlier version of Chapter 4 was published as "American Technological Assistance, Technology Transfers and Taiwan's Drive for Defense Self-Sufficiency," *Journal of Northeast Asian Studies* 8, no. 3 (Fall 1989), and an earlier version of Chapter 6 was published as "China's Threat to Taiwan," *Pacific Review* 5, no. 3 (1992). I thank the publishers for their permission to use this material.

Introduction

Taiwan is situated between Japan and the Philippines and lies approximately 100 miles off the coast of the great land mass of Asia. At 14,000 square miles, it is roughly the size of the state of West Virginia. The island is home to 20 million people, 14 million motor vehicles, and the government of the Republic of China (ROC or Taiwan).

Charles Maynes, editor of *Foreign Policy*, has noted that "the world has arrived at one of those rare periods in history when everything seems to change."[1] Taiwan is a case in point. Martial law has been lifted, opposition parties have formed, and the government has ended its ban on economic and cultural exchanges with the People's Republic of China (PRC). On the international front, Taipei is seeking to rejoin international organizations, strengthen its substantive ties with other states, and join any collective security system that might emerge in post-Cold War Asia. Despite these extraordinary changes, however, Taiwan's unique position in the international community means that its security will continue to rest primarily on two

its relations with the United States.[2]   Indeed, the PRC has
repeatedly refused to renounce the use of force to take Taiwan,
and there is little prospect that any new international order will
enhance Taiwan's security.

THE FOCUS

This book is an introductory study of the complex security
relationship that exists between the United States and Taiwan. It
shows how US security policy toward Taiwan has been steered
primarily by Cold War calculations and how provisions for
America's security relationship with Taiwan are principally
outlined in two contradictory documents: the Taiwan Relations
Act and the US-PRC Joint Communiqué of 1982. It also explains
how the US has employed these apparent inconsistencies in policy
to its own advantage. In conclusion, this study suggests that with
the disintegration of the Soviet Union and the end of the Cold
War, the time has arrived for the US to make some adjustments
in its relations with Taiwan.   These modifications, however,
should not include a change in American security policy toward
Taiwan. It is likely that the current policy—a strategy that was
carefully crafted during the Cold War—will continue to serve
American interests in a post-Cold War environment.

THE SCOPE

This study covers the period from 1949, a watershed year in
America's relations with the ROC, to 1992. Before 1949, the
ROC retained at least some modicum of control over portions of
mainland China, but afterward it was confined to the island of
Taiwan and several small islets.
The book focuses on America's security relationship with the
ROC.   Washington's military links with Beijing or other
governments are discussed only as they relate to America's

security relationship with Taiwan. Moreover, primary emphasis is placed on America's security ties with Taiwan after the normalization of diplomatic relations with the PRC in 1979.

THE ORGANIZATION

The first two chapters provide readers with an introduction to Taiwan. Chapter 1 serves as a historical overview and discusses the island's extraordinary economic and political development. Chapter 2 examines US-ROC strategic relations during the Cold War. Although many factors undoubtedly contributed to the making of US policy, the chapter shows how America's relationship with Taiwan has been steered primarily by Cold War considerations.

The next three chapters analyze current American policy toward the security of Taiwan. Chapter 3 explains how US policy is principally outlined in the Taiwan Relations Act (TRA) and the US-PRC Joint Communiqué of 1982, and explores the terms, nuances and significance of each agreement. Chapter 4 examines American technology transfers to Taiwan—a major loophole in the 1982 Communiqué—and Taiwan's drive for defense self-sufficiency. Chapter 5 explores the Bush administration's decision in 1992 to lift the decade-old ban on the sale of F–16 aircraft to Taiwan and discusses whether this move violates US policy.

Chapter 6 assesses the PRC's security threat to Taiwan. It suggests that while a conjunction of several long-term trends is combining to lessen mainland China's security threat to Taiwan, the possibility of conflict still exists. Chapter 7 should be of particular interest to policymakers. It examines various options open to an administration if it wishes to change, alter, or otherwise revise US policy toward the security of Taiwan. Chapter 8, the concluding chapter, briefly summarizes the evolution of American policy and suggests that the time has arrived for the United States to make some adjustments in its relations with Taiwan. These modifications, however, should not include a change in America's security relationship with Taiwan.

Notes

1. Charles William Maynes, "America without the Cold War," *Foreign Policy*, no. 78 (Spring 1990): 3.
2. See Emerson Niou, "An Analysis of the Republic of China's Security Issues," *Issues and Studies* 28, no.1, (January 1992): 94.

1

Economic and Political Development in Taiwan

Taiwan is a place of paradoxes and contradictions. The Republic of China (ROC) still claims to be the sole, legitimate government of China, but it exercises effective control over only the island of Taiwan and several small islets. With just 20 million people, the country nevertheless has the world's largest foreign exchange reserves (over US $87 billion) and is the world's fourteenth largest trader. It was a founding member of the United Nations, yet it no longer belongs to that organization or maintains formal diplomatic relations with any of the world's leading powers.

HISTORICAL OVERVIEW

The Ching dynasty (1644–1911) administered the island of Taiwan as a prefecture of the mainland China province of Fukien (Fujian) from 1683 until 1886, when Taiwan became a separate province of China. In 1895, following China's defeat in the first Sino-Japanese War, Taiwan was formally ceded to the Empire of

Japan by the Treaty of Shimonoseki. For the next 50 years, Taiwan was ruled by Japan.

On December 11, 1943, the US, the United Kingdom and the ROC issued a communiqué stating that it was their intention to return Taiwan to China. This agreement eventually came to be known as the Cairo Declaration. Specifically, the communiqué stated:

Japan shall be stripped of all the islands in the Pacific which she has seized or occupied since the beginning of the First World War in 1914, and that all territories Japan has stolen from the Chinese, such as Manchuria, Formosa and the Pescadores, shall be restored to the Republic of China.[1]

The Soviet Union approved the declaration four days later at the Tehran Conference. On July 26, 1945, the leaders of the US, the UK and the ROC declared in the Potsdam Proclamation that "the terms of the Cairo Declaration shall be carried out and Japanese sovereignty shall be limited to the islands of Honshu, Hokkaido, Kyushu, Shikoku and such minor islands as we determine."[2] Shortly afterward, the Soviet Union and France indicated that they would also adhere to the Potsdam Proclamation. When World War II ended, "the Supreme Commander of the Allied Powers gave the Nationalist government of Chiang Kai-shek authority to accept the Japanese surrender and administer the island."[3]

When ROC armed forces liberated Taiwan in 1945, the native inhabitants initially welcomed them. Soon, however, they discovered that the military was largely an undisciplined mob intent on robbing and looting the local population. Their hatred was intensified by certain measures enacted by the new governing authorities:

The Nationalist official in charge, Chen Yi, quickly seized all Japanese property, public and private, which the Taiwanese had hoped would revert to them, and considerable Taiwanese property as well. He and his underlings shipped large stocks of raw materials, factory machinery, Japanese military supplies, and even metals from buildings and the telegraph system to Hong Kong and Shanghai, where they sold them at large personal profit. They held wealthy Taiwanese for ransom and stole outright from the poor.[4]

On February 28, 1947, a group of Taiwanese rebelled against ROC authority. According to most accounts (including the official US government report), mainland troops overreacted to the crisis and massacred many innocent civilians:

The economic deterioration of the island and the administration of the mainland officials became so bad that on February 28, 1947, popular resentment erupted into a major rebellion. In the ensuing days the Government put down the revolt in a series of military actions which cost thousands of lives. Order was restored but the hatred of the mainland Chinese was increased.[5]

The killings poisoned relations between mainlanders (those who arrived in Taiwan after 1945) and native Taiwanese (those who arrived in Taiwan before 1945) for many years to come. Only recently, after more than 40 years, has the ROC government apologized to the victims of the "2-28 incident."

In 1949, after suffering a series of major defeats on the mainland, the Kuomintang (KMT) government of China retreated to the island of Taiwan. As might be expected, the influx of almost 2 million troops, government bureaucrats and refugees was a severe strain on the island's limited resources. But it was widely believed that this situation was only transitory; Taiwan would serve either as Generalissimo Chiang Kai-shek's last stand against Communist Chinese forces or as a staging area to retake the mainland. No one imagined that the Nationalist government would remain in Taipei for almost half a century:

When we retreated to Taiwan in 1949, we never thought that we would be here for 40 years. Either we would take back the mainland or the Communists would have to kill us all. One way or another, we thought the thing would be resolved.[6]

Following the outbreak of hostilities in Korea in June 1950, President Harry S. Truman ordered the US Seventh Fleet to neutralize the Taiwan Strait. With China's entry into the Korean War, US support for Taiwan became firm policy. These moves probably spared the KMT forces on Taiwan and helped lay the groundwork for the ensuing economic and political miracles.

The Economic Miracle

In 1954, a secret national intelligence estimate of Taiwan conducted by the American government concluded that "Taiwan no longer has a viable economy."[7] At roughly the same time, Chiang Kai-shek came to the conclusion that his forces would not be able to recover mainland China militarily. Consequently, he agreed to transform Taiwan into a model province and thereby prove the superiority of the KMT's road to modernization. Chiang would employ political, rather than military, means to retake China.

By following what has sometimes been referred to as a mixed economic system, with heavy industries owned by the government and virtually all light industries, services and trading firms owned by private concerns, and with the US playing the roles of adviser, benefactor and protector (a role that it continues to assume to this day), Taiwan's economy took off. Between 1950 and 1991, the gross national product increased over 1000 percent, the economic growth rate averaging 9.15 percent in the 1960s, 10.26 percent in the 1970s and 8.25 percent in the 1980s (Table 1.1). During this same period, the benefits of Taiwan's economic miracle were spread fairly evenly through society; in terms of the Gini income concentration ratio, the gap between the highest and lowest 20 percent of the wage earners is less than that which exists in the United States.[8] The composition of Taiwan's labor force, a statistical characteristic that is often employed as a measure of national industrialization and modernization, reveals that the island's labor force began to experience a significant shift during the 1950s and 1960s. Whereas during the early 1950s approximately 52 percent of the labor force was engaged in agriculture and 20 percent in industry, by the early 1980s the percentage engaged in agriculture had dropped to 19 percent, while the ranks of those employed in industry had swollen to 42 percent.[9]

By the early 1990s, Taiwan had evolved into an economic powerhouse. In 1992, the island had a per capita income of US $8,815, a gross national product of US $180 billion and foreign reserves of approximately US $87 billion—the highest in the world.[10] Table 1.2 outlines the growth in per capita income in Taiwan between 1952 and 1991. As America's sixth largest trading partner—its bilateral trade with the US is more than the trade level between the US and mainland China—Taiwan commands the respect of America's political and financial leaders. Table 1.3 shows Taiwan's ranking in exports, imports and two-way trade during 1991.

The Political Miracle

Taiwan's economic development has received a lot of media attention. Much less publicized—but perhaps even more spectacular—is the country's political development. Frederick Frey once defined political development as "changes in the direction of greater distribution and reciprocity of power."[11] If we accept this definition, the ROC on Taiwan may be considered a model of political development. Since the early 1980s, it has made remarkable strides toward increased political participation and freedom:

Taiwan unquestionably has the institutional prerequisites of a democratic system. Freedom of speech, assembly and association exist, as does a highly literate and politically aware electorate with many sources of information available to it. The government has shown its willingness to conduct a dialogue with its critics through

Table 1.1
ROC Gross National Product: 1952–1991 (in Constant 1986 NT Millions of Dollars)

YEAR	AMOUNT	REAL GROWTH RATE(%)
1952	162,057	12.0
1955	209,842	8.1
1960	290,221	6.4
1961	310,060	6.8
1962	334,516	7.9
1963	365.823	9.4
1964	410,794	12.3
1965	456,028	11.0
1966	496,944	9.0
1967	549,661	10.6
1968	599,819	9.1
1969	654,093	9.0
1970	728,144	11.3
1971	822,856	13.0
1972	932,932	13.4
1973	1,052,206	12.8
1974	1,064,383	1.2
1975	1,111,623	4.4
1976	1,263,966	13.7
1977	1,393,583	10.3
1978	1,588,582	14.0
1979	1,722,896	8.5
1980	1,845,562	7.1
1981	1,951,825	5.8
1982	2,030,908	4.1
1983	2,206,506	8.7
1984	2,462,301	11.6
1985	2,599,001	5.6
1986	2,925,772	12.6
1987	3,273,073	11.9
1988	3,529,708	7.8
1989	3,788,485	7.3
1990	3,978,720	5.0
1991	4,270,073	7.3

Source: Council for Economic Planning and Development, Republic of China, *Taiwan Statistical Data Book, 1992* (Taipei: Council for Economic Planning and Development, July 1992), p. 36.

Table 1.2
ROC Per Capita National Income: 1952–1991 (in Constant 1986 NT Dollars)

YEAR	AMOUNT	REAL GROWTH RATE(%)
1952	18,345	9.2
1955	21.373	4.6
1960	24.589	2.1
1961	25.408	3.3
1962	26,774	5.4
1963	28,798	7.6
1964	31,705	10.1
1965	33,386	5.3
1966	35,466	6.2
1967	38,286	8.0
1968	40,832	6.6
1969	43,874	7.5
1970	47,710	8.7
1971	52,561	10.2
1972	58,439	11.2
1973	64,313	10.1
1974	62,331	-3.1
1975	63,428	1.8
1976	71,572	12.8
1977	76,813	7.3
1978	84,316	9.8
1979	89,604	6.3
1980	92,098	2.8
1981	94,374	2.5
1982	96,944	2.7
1983	104,130	7.4
1984	114,903	10.3
1985	119,581	4.1
1986	137,992	15.4
1987	154,838	12.2
1988	164,229	6.1
1989	174,407	6.2
1990	180,053	3.2
1991	192,693	7.0

Source: Ibid.

Table 1.3

Taiwan's Ranking in Exports, Imports and Two-Way Trade, 1991

Exporters	Importers	Two-Way Trade
1. USA	1. USA	1. USA
2. Germany	2. Germany	2. Germany
3. Japan	3. Japan	3. Japan
4. France	4. France	4. France
5. UK	5. UK	5. UK
6. Italy	6. Italy	6. Italy
7. Netherlands	7. Canada	7. Netherlands
8. Canada	8. Netherlands	8. Canada
9. Belgium & Luxembourg	9. Belgium & Luxembourg	9. Belgium & Luxembourg
10.Hong Kong	10.Hong Kong	10.Hong Kong
11.USSR	11.Spain	11.South Korea
12.Taiwan	12.South Korea	12.Spain
13.PRC	13.USSR	13.USSR
14.South Korea	14.Switzerland	14.Taiwan
15.Switzerland	15.Singapore	15.PRC
16.Spain	16.PRC	16.Switzerland
17.Singapore	17.Taiwan	17.Singapore

Source: Council Overview of Development in International Trade and the Trading System, GATT, (as reported in "Taiwan is 14th Largest Trader," *China Post* (International Airmail Edition), March 24, 1992, p. 1).

such forms as the National Affairs Conference. There are no perfect democratic systems. In the ROC, as elsewhere, improvements could be made, and are being made.[12]

Prior to 1949, there had never been an island-wide election on Taiwan. In 1951, the first such election was held in order to elect a provincial assembly. In subsequent years, elections were held on both the provincial and national levels. It was in the latter area that elections proved to be a vexing problem. Unable to conduct nationwide elections due to the Communists' occupation of mainland territories, the national government in 1948 enacted the Temporary Provisions Effective During the Period of Communist Rebellion. The Temporary Provisions essentially froze all nationally elected officials in their respective offices until such time as elections could be held on the mainland. Nevertheless, supplementary elections began to be held in 1969 for the purpose of electing new members to the National Assembly (electoral college), Legislative Yuan (legislature), and Control Yuan (an impeachment, censure and audit branch of government). Consequently, the number of locally elected officials grew steadily as time took its toll on older members.

Although Taiwan began to assume some of the characteristics of a democracy during the 1950s and 1960s, President Chiang Kai-shek continued to rule the island with an iron fist. Meaningful political reform began only after his charismatic son, Chiang Ching-kuo, became President in 1978. Since that time, Taiwan has undergone a metamorphosis.

In 1987, martial law was lifted, the print media deregulated and opposition political parties were allowed to form.[13] In 1989, the government allowed opposition parties to compete in Taiwan's Legislative Yuan elections. This election, which came only months after the bloody crackdown in Tiananmen Square, enabled the world to compare Taipei's commitment to democracy with the PRC's hardline response to popular demands for democratic reform. Representative Stephen Solarz (Democrat–New York), renowned for his criticism of the ROC government and support for Taiwanese dissidents, praised the electoral process:

The entire world can see the contrast between Taiwan and the PRC. In the PRC, when the people ask for democracy, they are greeted with a hail of bullets, and Beijing is drowned in a river of blood. In Taiwan, when people demand democracy, they are given an opportunity to participate in an electoral process and can vote for the candidates of their choice.[14]

Despite the inevitable tensions that accompany the democratization process—including demonstrations, brawls in the legislature and other disorders—the government's commitment to democratization remains firm. Indeed, since 1989, political reform on Taiwan has accelerated. In 1991, the last of the senior parliamentarians—commonly called the "old thieves"—were forced to retire. Several months later, the ROC conducted its first general elections in 40 years to elect a new National Assembly, the body that will revise the ROC's 1947 Constitution. In December 1992, general elections were held to elect a new 161-seat Legislative Yuan, the first ever to be chosen in its entirety by the Taiwanese people. Although the ruling KMT retained control of the island's legislature, the Democratic Progressive Party (DPP) made significant gains. The KMT won 96 seats, the DPP took 50 seats, the Chinese Social Democratic Party won 1 seat and independent candidates won 14. Commenting on the DPP's surprisingly strong showing, Jason Hu, Director-General of the ROC's Government Information Office, observed that "in most Asian countries, such as Japan, there's one dominant party and then some smaller parties, but instead of that we're seeing the possibility of a true bipartisan democracy on Taiwan."[15]

Notes

1. "Conference of President Roosevelt, Generalissimo Chiang Kai-shek and Prime Minister Churchill in North Africa," *Department of State Bulletin*, December 4, 1943, p. 393.
2. "Proclamation Defining Terms for Japanese Surrender," *Department of State Bulletin*, July 29, 1945, p. 137.
3. Chiao Chiao Hsieh, *Strategy For Survival* (London: Sherwood Press, 1985), p. 24.
4. Hill Gates, *Chinese Working Class Lives: Getting By in Taiwan* (Ithaca: Cornell University Press, 1987), p. 45.
5. *United States Relations with China* (Washington, D.C.: Department of State Division of Publications, Office of Public Affairs, August 1949), p. 308.

6. Author's private discussion with a high-ranking ROC military officer (now retired).

7. See "National Intelligence Estimate, September 14, 1954," in *US Department of State, Foreign Relations of the United States: 1952-1954, Vol. 14: China and Japan, Part I* (Washington, D.C.: US Government Printing Office, 1985), p. 634.

8. For more information, see Senator Paul Simon (Democrat–Illinois), "Proposals to Revitalize US Policy in Asia," *Congressional Record*, May 20, 1991, p. S6124.

9. See Chu-yuan Cheng, "Economic Development in Taiwan and Mainland China: A Comparison of Strategies and Performance," *Asian Affairs* (Spring 1983): pp. 69-70.

10. For more information, see "ROC Per Capita Income Ranks 25th in the World," *China Post* (International Airmail Edition), March 3, 1992, p. 3.

11. Quoted from Samuel P. Huntington, "Political Development and Political Decay," *World Politics* 17, no. 3, (April 1965): 388.

12. See Prepared Statement of Professor June Teufel Dreyer in *Taiwan: The Upcoming National Assembly Elections*, Hearing Before the Subcommittee on Asian and Pacific Affairs of the Committee on Foreign Affairs, House of Representatives, 102d Congress, 1st Session, September 24, 1991, p. 37.

13. Prior to 1987, opposition parties did exist. However, these parties—funded and supported by the KMT—could not be considered opposition parties. For more information on this sort of political activity, see Arthur J. Lerman, *Taiwan's Politics: The Provincial Assemblyman's World* (Washington, D.C.: University Press of America, 1978).

14. Nicholas Kristof, "Taiwan Opposition Claims Major Election Victory," *International Herald Tribune*, December 4, 1989, p. 2.

15. Nicholas D. Kristof, "Taiwan Election Helps Opposition," *New York Times*, December 20, 1992, p. 7.

2

The United States, Taiwan and the Cold War

Generalissimo Chiang Kai-shek and his Kuomintang government retreated to the island of Taiwan in 1949. Since that time, America's relations with the ROC have passed through several phases. Indeed, some have argued that American policy toward Taiwan "has gone through a complete cycle that started with relative indifference, moved to active support, and finally returned to relative benign neglect and indifference."[1] The discussion below examines each of these stages and shows how strategic considerations played a critical role in shaping American policy toward Taiwan.

U.S.-ROC ALLIANCE

During the early months of 1950, it appeared that Taiwan would be overrun by PRC forces. The US government, however, refused to assist the ROC in its efforts to repel Communist aggression. On January 5, 1950, President Harry S. Truman stated unequivocally that the United States would not become involved in the Chinese Civil War:

The United States has no predatory designs on Formosa or on any other Chinese territory. The United States has no desire to obtain special rights or to establish military bases on Formosa at this time. Nor does it have any intention of utilizing its armed forces to interfere in the present situation. The United States will not pursue a course which will lead to involvement in the civil conflict in China. Similarly, the United States government will not provide military aid or suggestions to Nationalist forces on Formosa.[2]

On April 10, 1950, the US Central Intelligence Agency reported that "the fall of Taiwan before the end of 1950 still seems the most likely course of future developments."[3] On May 17, following the fall of Hainan Island and the unexpected evacuation of the Chussan islands, the American Chargé in China informed the Secretary of State that "[the] fate of Taiwan [is] sealed."[4] Two days later, the Department of State advised all Americans to withdraw from Taiwan as soon as possible.[5] It was during this atmosphere of crisis that members of the Truman administration seriously began to formulate plans to safeguard Taiwan's existence independent of the Communist mainland.

It is highly improbable that these efforts were motivated by any great desire to save the neck of Chiang or other members of the KMT. President Truman and many of the members of his administration held both Chiang and his followers in contempt.[6] Even General Douglas MacArthur, often viewed as a great friend and defender of the Generalissimo, privately argued that the administration should encourage Chiang to return to the mainland because "it might be a good idea to let him land and get rid of him that way."[7]

The pressures that mounted from within the administration for a revision of American policy toward Taiwan may be traced primarily to the geopolitical significance of the island. Taiwan is situated just off the coast of the great land mass of Asia and links the Indian and Pacific oceans. Its strategic importance has not been lost on military planners and strategists ranging from the Imperial Japanese high command, who chose the island as a staging area for their invasion of the Philippines, to General MacArthur, who referred to Taiwan as an "unsinkable aircraft carrier." Increasingly, members of the American military argued that although Taiwan would not necessarily enhance American military capabilities in East Asia, it would certainly enhance the military capabilities of any power hostile to the United States.[8] Therefore, they believed that it would be wise policy to take such actions as necessary to deny the island to a hostile power. Interestingly, this perceived importance of the island was not lost on the KMT and may have been one of the primary reasons that it elected to retreat to Taiwan. During a KMT meeting held on April 8, 1949, ROC Foreign Minister George Yeh "indicated that since the US is thought to consider Taiwan an essential line in its Western Pacific defense chain, there was little likelihood that it would be allowed to fall to the Reds."[9] Shortly after this meeting, the KMT government retreated to Taiwan.

Contrary to the popular misconception, members of the Truman administration began to develop plans to deny Taiwan to the Chinese Communists prior to the outbreak of hostilities in Korea. Some of the most interesting plans in this area were formulated by Dean Rusk, then Assistant Secretary of State for Far Eastern Affairs. On May 30, 1950, Rusk sent a memo to Secretary of State Dean Acheson outlining what could perhaps best be described as a crude domino theory approach to the Taiwan situation. Rusk argued that if the administration did not soon draw a line against Communist expansion in Asia, "we can expect an accelerated deterioration of our influence in the Mediterranean, Near East, Asia and the Pacific."[10] He went on to state that Taiwan would provide the US with an ideal place to draw such a line. Rusk's plan to accomplish this drawing of the line bears a striking similarity to the policy that would be adopted by the US government several weeks later:

If the United States were to announce that it would neutralize Formosa, not permitting it either to be taken by the communists or to be used as a base of military operations against the mainland, that is a decision that we could certainly maintain, short of open war by the Soviet Union. Everyone knows that to be the case.[11]

Although calls for a change in US policy toward Taiwan accelerated during early 1950, it was only after the outbreak of the Korean conflict on June 25, 1950 that the Truman administration openly reversed its position. On June 27, the President announced that he had ordered the Seventh Fleet to "neutralize" the Taiwan Strait, thereby intervening in the Chinese Civil War.[12] As John Kuan observed, "The Korean War transformed American policy from abandonment of the Republic of China to the defense of Taiwan."[13]

It is noteworthy that even during the early stages of the Korean War, Truman's attitude toward the KMT Chinese who had retreated to Taiwan could be characterized as anything but sympathetic. The President is reported to have mused openly over the possibility of returning Taiwan to the Japanese or the feasibility of replacing Generalissimo Chiang Kai-shek with General Douglas MacArthur.[14] However, the PRC's entry into the Korean conflict in October 1950 led American support for KMT forces to become firm policy.

Between 1950 and 1968 (when US financial aid was terminated), massive amounts of military and economic aid poured into Taiwan (Table 2.1). ROC officials acknowledge that the island "benefitted a lot from the generous economic aid from the US."[15] Furthermore, the two governments concluded a mutual defense treaty in 1954. For over two decades following Senate ratification of the treaty, the US maintained a firm alliance with the ROC.

Table 2.1
U.S. Economic Aid to Taiwan: 1951–1968 (Millions of U.S.
Dollars)

FY	Total Arrival Amount	Nonproject Assistance	Project Assistance
1951-54	375.2	300.4	74.8
1955	132.0	96.4	35.6
1956	101.6	69.5	32.1
1957	108.1	66.2	42.9
1958	81.6	51.9	29.7
1959	128.9	73.7	55.2
1960	101.1	68.7	32.4
1961	94.2	70.4	23.8
1962	65.9	59.3	6.6
1963	115.3	113.5	1.8
1964	83.9	37.3	46.6
1965	56.5	56.1	0.4
1966	4.2	4.2	----
1967	4.4	4.4	----
1968	29.3	29.3	----
TOTAL	1,482.2	1,100.3	381.9

Source: Council for Economic Planning and Development, Republic of
China. Information provided courtesy of Moses Lu, Information
Division, Coordination Council for North American Affairs, Chicago.

THE NIXON INITIATIVE AND
U.S.-PRC RAPPROCHEMENT

During the late 1960s, a variety of geopolitical and strategic
considerations led President Richard M. Nixon to seek a
rapprochement with the PRC. As early as 1967, he had hinted
at the need for a change in America's China policy. In an article
for *Foreign Affairs*, Nixon wrote of a need to end China's "angry
isolation" and called for measures that would succeed in "pulling
China back into the world community."[16] Immediately after
accepting the 1968 Republican nomination for President, Nixon
reiterated that "we must not forget China. We must always seek

opportunities to talk with her, as with the USSR. . . . We must
not only watch for changes. We must seek to make changes."[17]
Shortly after assuming the presidency in 1969, Nixon began to
chart a new course for America's China policy.

Having inherited an unpopular, divisive and seemingly endless
conflict in Vietnam from his predecessor, thoughts of an
honorable settlement to the war were foremost among Nixon's
concerns. The rapprochement with China was viewed initially as
a means by which the US could indirectly coerce the recalcitrant
North Vietnamese government to the peace talks. Indeed,
Nixon's initiative toward China might be characterized as an
indirect two-pronged attack upon North Vietnam. First, by
mending relations with Beijing, Nixon hoped that he might
succeed in convincing Chinese authorities to reduce support for
North Vietnam and "assist America in pressuring Hanoi to agree
upon a settlement of the Vietnam War."[18]   Second, the
maneuver was intended to disturb the Soviet Union and provide
it with an incentive to pressure Hanoi into a negotiated settlement.

Nixon believed that "the greatest incentive for Soviet
cooperation in Vietnam, was our new relationship with the
Chinese."[19]   When meeting with Soviet Ambassador Anatoly
Dobrynin in 1969, the President pointedly reminded him that "the
only beneficiary of US-Soviet disagreement over Vietnam is
China."[20] Thus, Nixon began a practice whereby time and again
American Presidents would resort to threatening the Soviet Union
with the so-called China card.

Nixon's opening to China must be considered as much more
than simply an innovative attempt to push the Soviet Union and
China into playing an ancillary role in America's scheme for an
honorable resolution to the Vietnam conflict. Global strategic
concerns also played a major role, and over time, these
considerations would take precedence over the short-range
objective of a respectable Vietnam settlement.

Throughout the 1960s, the strength and projection capabilities
of the Soviet Union's conventional and strategic forces grew
significantly. As a result, the PRC gradually came to be viewed

"as a desirable counterweight to the Soviet Union which was rapidly gaining strategic nuclear parity with the United States."[21] Moreover, Henry Kissinger and other administration officials believed that America's new relationship with the PRC might compel the Soviets into concessions on the Strategic Arms Limitations Talks (SALT I) and other matters. Finally, Nixon judged that it was not in America's national interest to be at odds permanently with a hostile and increasingly powerful nuclear power.[22]

For its own part, the PRC had ample motivation to abandon its dual-adversary strategy toward the superpowers and pursue a policy of détente (or perhaps even a united front) with the United States. The 1960s had witnessed an escalation in Sino-Soviet tensions. The 1968 Soviet invasion of Czechoslovakia and the subsequent proclamation of the Brezhnev Doctrine were a cause of great concern in Beijing. But most alarming was the 1969 Sino-Soviet border crisis. The ultimate effect of this crisis, a confrontation that led to a direct clash between Chinese and Soviet forces, proved to be "genuine panic in China, at both the elite and popular levels."[23]

The series of historic steps that began with the PRC's expressed desire to resume the Sino-American talks in Warsaw and led ultimately to Nixon's visit to China and the signing of the 1972 Shanghai Communiqué have been extensively documented elsewhere. However, it is noteworthy that the communiqué contained a thinly veiled threat directed against the Soviet Union. In what is sometimes referred to as the "anti-hegemony clause" of the document, both governments pledged that neither party "should seek hegemony in Asia Pacific region and each is opposed to efforts by any other country or group of countries to establish hegemony."[24]

As the PRC came to play a greater role in America's containment strategy, the relative importance of Taiwan declined. Indicative of this change, in 1971 the US quietly acquiesced to Taiwan's expulsion from the United Nations, and it no longer supported Taipei's efforts to maintain formal diplomatic ties with

other governments. Commenting on Taiwan's precarious
international position at the time, Immanuel Hsu wrote that
Taiwan was becoming "increasingly isolated" and that "its future
international status looks uncertain."[25]

NORMALIZATION OF U.S.–PRC RELATIONS

A variety of domestic political considerations (the Watergate
scandal, the Panama Canal Treaty, the death of Mao, and the
arrest of the Gang of Four, among others) caused the US-PRC
normalization process to stall during the mid-1970s. In 1979,
however, the Carter administration established diplomatic
relations with Beijing. According to Zbigniew Brzezinski, then
National Security Advisor, the decision to formalize ties with the
PRC was "definitely influenced by the Soviet dimension."[26]
US-PRC rapprochement was viewed as a means by which
Washington could counterbalance Moscow's military buildup.
The US also hoped that the normalization decision would
positively influence the progress of the SALT II negotiations and
help "Moscow understand the value of restraint and
reciprocity."[27] In sum, US officials hoped that "perhaps if the
Soviets worry a little more about our policy toward China, we
will have less cause to worry about our relations with the
Soviets."[28]

In order to achieve normalization, the Carter administration
agreed to accede to Beijing's long-standing conditions for
diplomatic relations: the "derecognition" of the ROC, the
termination of the US-ROC Mutual Defense Treaty, and the
withdrawal of all US forces stationed on Taiwan. These moves
came as a devastating blow to Taiwan. However, the US did
agree to maintain "unofficial" or "substantive" relations with
Taipei.

During the post-normalization period, US-Taiwan relations
would be guided by the Taiwan Relations Act (TRA), a highly
unusual piece of legislation drafted by members of the US

Congress, passed by an overwhelming majority in both houses and subsequently signed into law by President Carter. The law provides for continued American commercial and cultural relations with Taiwan. It also outlines the terms of America's security commitment to Taiwan (see Chapter 3). During the early 1980s, the Reagan administration sought to patch up its differences with Beijing and establish some sort of tacit alliance directed against Soviet expansionism. On August 17, 1982, President Reagan and the government of the PRC issued a joint communiqué focusing on the overall issue of continued US arms transfers to Taiwan. This document seemed to contradict the TRA by committing the US to a gradual reduction in its military support for Taiwan (see Chapter 3).

CONCLUSION

Sidney Verba once observed that "no model and no theorist, no matter how committed to holistic principles, can encompass the totality of a situation."[29] The same observation applies when one attempts to explain shifts and swings in American policy toward Taiwan. During the 1950s, domestic political considerations—strong congressional and public support for Taipei—played a role in shaping America's China policy.[30] In the 1970s, economic concerns—particularly the allure of the so-called China market—contributed to the Carter administration's decision to normalize relations with Beijing. The personality or personal characteristics of individual American decisionmakers, ranging from John Foster Dulles to Jimmy Carter, may also have some explanatory value. In short, many factors influenced the development of American policy toward the two Chinas.

Although numerous considerations contributed to the making of US policy, strategic concerns were the driving force. The outbreak of the Korean War—a conflict viewed by many as the first step in a Communist drive for world conquest—led the US into an alliance with the ROC on Taiwan. Years later, a growing

Soviet threat led Washington to downgrade relations with Taipei and conclude what Brzezinski described as "a defacto alliance or, if you will, an alliance by stealth, between the United States and China."[31] In sum, "military cooperation between the US and China to counter the Soviet threat was the raison d'etre of the Washington-Beijing rapprochement."[32]

Government authorities in Taipei acknowledge the paramount role that strategic considerations have played in the triangular relationship between Washington, Beijing and Taipei. Fredrick Chien, Foreign Minister of the Republic of China, has offered the following observation:

Strategic factors brought the US and the mainland together. In the late 1960s, the US learned that the USSR was targeting missiles against mainland Chinese positions. That is what made it possible for Kissinger to make his secret visit to the mainland. This triangular strategic configuration also played an important role in the final normalization of relations between the PRC and the US. And, strategic considerations were important with respect to the August 17, 1982 communiqué.[33]

By the early 1980s, US policy toward Taiwan had gone through a complete cycle.

Notes

1. See Daniel Metraux, *Taiwan's Political and Economic Growth in the Late Twentieth Century* (New York: Edwin Mellen Press, 1991), p. 95.
2. See "The President's News Conference on January 5, 1950," in *Public Papers of the President of the US: Harry S. Truman* (Washington, D.C.: U.S. Government Printing Office, 1965), p. 11.
3. See "Memorandum by the Assistant Secretary of State for Far Eastern Affairs (Rusk) to the Secretary of State, April 17, 1950," in US Department of State, *Foreign Relations of the United States: 1950, vol.*

6 (Washington, D.C.: US Government Printing Office, 1976), p. 330 (hereafter cited as *FR 1950* vol. 6).

4. "The Chargé in China (Strong) to the Secretary of State, May 17, 1950," in *FR 1950,* vol. 6 p. 340.

5. "The Acting Secretary of State to the Embassy in China, May 19, 1950," in Ibid, p. 343.

6. Years after his retirement from the presidency, Truman stated that "I never changed my mind about Chiang and his gang . . . every damn one of them ought to be in jail, and I'd like to live to see the day they are." Quoted from Merle Miller, *Plain Speaking: An Oral Biography of Harry S. Truman* (New York: G. P. Putnam, 1974), p. 283.

7. "Extracts of a Memorandum of Conversations by Mr. W. Averell Harriman, Special Assistant to the President, with General Douglas MacArthur in Tokyo on August 6 and 8, 1950," in *FR 1950,* vol. 6, p. 428.

8. See John Lewis Gaddis, "The Strategic Perspective: The Rise and Fall of the Defensive Perimeter Concept, 1947–1950," in Dorothy Borg and Waldo Heinrichs (eds.), *Uncertain Years: Chinese-American Relations, 1947–1950* (New York: Columbia University Press, 1980), pp. 81–93.

9. "The Minister-Counselor of Embassy in China (Clark) to the Secretary of State, April 8, 1949," in US Department of State, *Foreign Relations of the United States: 1949, vol. 8* (Washington, D.C.: US Government Printing Office, 1978), p. 234.

10. "Extract from a Draft Memorandum by the Assistant Secretary of State for Far Eastern Affairs (Rusk) to the Secretary of State, May 30, 1950," in *FR, 1950,* vol. 6, p. 349.

11. Ibid.

12. See "Statement by the President on the Situation in Korea," in *Public Papers,* p. 492.

13. See John C. Kuan, *A Review of US-ROC Relations, 1949-1978* (Taipei: Asia and World Institute, 1980), p. 10.

14. Joseph C. Goulden, *Korea: The Untold Story of the War* (New York: Times Books, 1982), p. 73.

15. Author's interview with Dr. Fredrick Chien, Foreign Minister of the Republic of China, Taipei, Taiwan, Republic of China, July 14, 1992.

16. See Richard M. Nixon, "Asia After Vietnam," *Foreign Affairs* 41, no. 1 (October 1967): 111–125.

17. Henry Kissinger, *The White House Years* (Boston: Little, Brown and Company, 1979), p. 164.

18. See Michael Schaller, *The United States and China in the Twentieth Century* (New York: Oxford University Press, 1979), p. 165.

19. Richard M. Nixon, *RN: The Memoirs of Richard Nixon* (New York: Warner Books, 1979), p. 511.

20. Ibid., p. 502.

21. Steven L. Levine, "The Soviet Factor in Sino-American Relations," in Michel Oksenberg and Robert B. Oxnam (eds.), *Dragon and Eagle—United States-China Relations: Past and Future* (New York: Basic Books, 1978), p. 247.

22. See Richard M. Nixon, *RN* pp. 461–462.

23. Harold Hinton, "The Sino-Soviet-US Triangle," in Stephen P. Gilbert (ed.), *Security in Northeast Asia: Approaching the Pacific Century* (Boulder, Colorado: Westview Press, 1988), p. 12.

24. For a complete text of the communiqué, see *China: US Policy Since 1945* (Washington, D.C.: Congressional Quarterly, 1980).

25. Immanuel C. Y. Hsu, *The Rise of Modern China* (New York: Oxford University Press, 1975), p. 932.

26. Zbigniew Brzezinski, *Power and Principle* (New York: Farrar, Straus and Giroux, 1983), p. 197.

27. Ibid. p. 196.

28. Ibid., p. 200.

29. Sidney Verba, "Assumptions of Rationality and Non-Rationality in Models of the International System," in Klause Knorr and Sidney Verba (eds.), *The International System* (Princeton: Princeton University Press, 1961), p. 106.

30. The activities of the pro-Taiwan "China lobby" might also have played a role. For more information, see Ross Y. Koen, *The China Lobby in American Politics* (New York: Harper and Row, 1974).

31. See Testimony of Zbigniew Brzezinski in *United States-China Relations: Today's Realities and Prospects for the Future*, Hearing Before the Committee on Foreign Relations, United States Senate, 98th Congress, 2d Session, May 17, 1984, p. 29.

32. See John F. Copper, *China Diplomacy: The Washington-Taipei-Beijing Triangle* (Boulder, Colorado: Westview Press, 1992), p. 50.

33. Interview with Chien.

3

United States Security
Ties to Taiwan:
Institutionalized Ambiguity

In 1979, the United States government recognized the People's Republic of China as the sole, legitimate government of all of China. In order to achieve normalization, the Carter administration agreed to accede to Beijing's three long-standing conditions for normalization: the "derecognition" of the Republic of China, the termination of the US-ROC Mutual Defense Treaty, and the withdrawal of all US forces stationed on Taiwan. At the same time, however, the US promised to continue to maintain commercial, cultural, and other relations with the authorities on Taiwan.

Since the formal abrogation of the US-ROC Mutual Defense Treaty in 1980, America's security relationship with Taiwan could best be described as ambiguous. Indeed, US policy is principally outlined in two contradictory documents: the Taiwan Relations Act (TRA) and the US-PRC Joint Communiqué of 1982 (see Appendixes 1 and 2).

THE TAIWAN RELATIONS ACT

On December 15, 1978, President Jimmy Carter, without any prior consultation with members of Congress, announced the establishment of full diplomatic relations between the United States and the PRC, to become effective January 1, 1979. However, approximately 55 treaties, agreements, and programs with Taiwan were to remain in effect, and President Carter declared that "the people of our country will maintain our current commercial, cultural, trade and other relations with Taiwan through non-governmental means."[1]

This highly unusual multilevel arrangement was unique and required legitimization by Congress.   Rejecting the Carter administration's legislative proposals as too timid, the Congress passed the TRA by an overwhelming majority, and the act was subsequently signed into law by the President.[2]

America's security commitment to Taiwan is outlined principally in Sections 2 and 3 of the TRA.   According to Section 2, it is the policy of the United States "to consider any attempt to resolve the Taiwan issue by other than peaceful means, including boycotts or embargoes, a threat to the peace and security of the Western Pacific area and of grave concern to the United States."[3]

In the event that Taiwan is threatened, Section 3 states:

The President is directed to inform the Congress promptly of any threat to the security or the social or economic system of the people on Taiwan and any danger to the interests of the US arising therefrom.   The President and the Congress shall determine, in accordance with constitutional processes, appropriate action by the US in response to any such danger.

In terms of American arms sales to Taiwan, the most pertinent passages of the TRA are to be found in Section 3:

(a)   In furtherance of the policy set forth in section 2 of this Act, the United States will make available to Taiwan such defense articles and defense services in such quantity as may be necessary to enable Taiwan to maintain a sufficient self-defense capability.

(b) The President and Congress shall determine the nature and quantity of such defense articles and services based solely upon their judgement of the needs of Taiwan, in accordance with procedures established by law. Such determination of Taiwan's defense needs shall include review by United States military authorities in connection with recommendations to the President and Congress.

The TRA clearly states that it is the policy of the United States government to provide Taiwan with such weapons as may be necessary for its security and an adequate defensive capability and that the quality and quantity of these weapons will be determined by the President and the Congress after consultation with US military authorities. Moreover, the House Committee on Foreign Affairs report on the TRA emphasized that "the United States will make available modern weapons for Taiwan, and not shift to a policy of supplying only obsolete weapons."[4] It is noteworthy that US arms transfers to Taiwan actually increased following the passage of the TRA; the US sold approximately $1.4 billion of weapons to Taiwan during the first four years following the passage of the act.[5]

Given Beijing's persistent refusal to rule out the use of force to take Taiwan, it is also significant that the TRA addresses the issue of Taiwan's future. In this respect, the most important provision is found in Section 2(b), which states that it is the policy of the US "to make clear that the United States decision to establish diplomatic relations with the People's Republic of China rests upon the expectation that the future of Taiwan will be determined by peaceful means." Furthermore, it is noteworthy that the law applies to: "the governing authorities on Taiwan recognized by the United States as the Republic of China prior to January 1, 1979, *and any successor governing authorities* (including political subdivisions, agencies, and instrumentalities thereof) [emphasis added]." It would appear, therefore, that any provisions for support of the ROC, as mandated by the TRA, would apply equally to an independent Republic of Taiwan so long as the law remained in effect.[6] However, the Department of State has emphasized that "neither the American Institute in Taiwan nor the State Department has ever made an official statement saying that once Taiwan becomes independent, the Taiwan Relations Act will still apply."[7]

THE U.S.-PRC JOINT COMMUNIQUÉ OF AUGUST 17, 1982

To some Americans—particularly the conservative wing of the Republican party—the Carter administration's provisions for the security of Taiwan were unsatisfactory. They charged that the Democratic President had "sold out" America's old friend and ally on Taiwan. As might be expected, the matter became a contentious issue during the 1980 presidential election campaign.

Ronald Reagan, the Republican candidate for President, criticized the Carter administration's handling of the normalization issue. He argued that the US had made unnecessary concessions to achieve normalization:

By accepting China's three conditions for "normalization" Jimmy Carter made concessions that Presidents Nixon and Ford had steadfastly refused to make. I was and am critical of his decision because I believe he made concessions that were not necessary and not in our national interest. I felt that a condition of normalization—by itself a sound policy choice—should have been the retention of a liaison office on Taiwan of equivalent status to the one which we had earlier established in Beijing.[8]

During the campaign, Reagan threatened to upgrade relations with Taiwan.

After assuming office in January 1981, President Reagan changed his position. Alexander Haig and other White House officials convinced Reagan that Beijing's continued strategic cooperation against Soviet expansionism outweighed any need to improve ties with Taipei.[9] In early 1981, the US Department of State said that formal relations with Taiwan would not be restored.[10] On January 11, 1982, officials announced that the administration would not sell Taiwan the FX fighter plane or other advanced military equipment because "no military need for such aircraft exists."[11] The most crushing blow for Taiwan, however, came several months later when Washington and Beijing concluded what came to be known as the August 17, 1982 US-PRC Joint Communiqué or Shanghai II. In this agreement, the US appeared to promise to reduce its arms sales to Taiwan.

On August 17, 1982, President Ronald Reagan and the government of the PRC issued a joint communiqué focusing on the overall issue of continued US arms transfers to the ROC. A passage from one particularly relevant paragraph is quoted below:

(6) The US government states that it does not seek to carry out a long term policy of arms sales to Taiwan and will not exceed, either in qualitative or in quantitative terms, the level of those supplied in recent years since the establishment of diplomatic relations between the United States and China, and that it intends to reduce gradually its sales of arms to Taiwan, leading over a period of time to a final resolution.[12]

Taken at face value, the document would appear to pledge the US to eschew long-term arms sales to Taiwan and to keep sales from exceeding either the quality or quantity of arms sold to Taiwan after the US established diplomatic relations with the PRC. The communiqué also apparently commits the US to reduce its arms sales to Taiwan gradually.

THE MEANINGS OF THE TWO DOCUMENTS

Does the TRA commit the US to Taiwan's defense? Does the 1982 US-PRC Joint Communiqué obligate the US to reduce its military support for Taiwan? In order to answer these questions, one must examine the various meanings, nuances and interpretations of the two documents.

The Taiwan Relations Act

Is the US committed to fight to protect Taiwan? In 1979, President Carter said in an interview that "a future President has the option of going to war and protecting Taiwan."[13] When questioned later about the remark, Carter replied, "I wanted to point out that no future decision by myself or my successor is prevented."[14] Members of the legislative branch have argued that the act is "tantamount to establishing an alliance with Taiwan that requires America to defend Taiwan against aggression."[15] Comments along similar lines have been made by American Presidents. In 1983, President Reagan said that "we in no way retreat from our alliance with and our friendship with the Chinese on Taiwan . . . they have been allies of our going all the way back to World War II."[16]

Some argue that "today the United States remains committed to the defense of Taiwan."[17] But these individuals are mistaken. The TRA provides the US only with an *option* to defend Taiwan; it does not necessarily commit the US to Taiwan's defense. The difference is important. The TRA is not a mutual defense treaty, and unlike America's existing security relationships with the Republic of Korea or Japan, a US response to hostilities directed against Taiwan is not guaranteed. Perhaps no one else has underscored this fact more than Dr. Chen Li-an, Taiwan's Defense Minister. When asked whether Taipei could depend on help from Washington in the event of an attack, Chen replied that the defense of Taiwan "is our [the ROC's] problem . . . [and] the ROC military must have the capability and strength to handle an attack on its own, without depending on outside help."[18]

The 1982 U.S.-PRC Joint Communiqué

Shortly before the issuance of the US-PRC Joint Communiqué, the US announced that it would sell Taiwan additional F-5E fighter aircraft. At roughly the same time, the administration gave several assurances to Taipei. These so-called Six Assurances are listed below:

1. The US has not agreed to set a date for ending arms sales to the ROC.
2. The US has not agreed to hold prior consultations with the Chinese Communists on arms sales to the ROC.
3. The US will not play any mediation role between Taipei and Beijing.
4. The US has not agreed to revise the TRA.
5. The US has not altered its position regarding sovereignty over Taiwan.
6. The US will not exert pressure on the ROC to enter into negotiations with the PRC.[19]

These moves, however, did little to reassure those who feared that Reagan had compromised Taiwan's security.

In order to deflect a rising groundswell of criticism following the release of the 1982 US-PRC Joint Communiqué, the Reagan administration, through public pronouncements and appearances before congressional hearings, attempted to clarify the meaning of the accord. During congressional hearings that followed the release of the communiqué, John H. Holdridge, then Assistant Secretary of the Bureau of East Asian and Pacific Affairs in the Department of State, testified that "what we have here is not a treaty or an agreement but a statement of future US policy [and] we fully intend to implement this policy in accordance with *our understanding* of it [emphasis added]."[20] Members of Congress were assured that arms sales would not automatically decrease and that the administration had not set any dollar limit on sales. Under the close questioning of Senator John Glenn (Democrat–Ohio), Holdridge refused to speculate as to whether

arms sales to the ROC would terminate in 10, 50, or even 100
years. Indeed, Holdridge's response to Senator Glenn's question
was that "your guess is as good as mine."[21] Administration
spokesmen also suggested that previous sales figures for arms
sales to Taiwan could eventually be adjusted by an inflation factor
and that, as a consequence, the actual dollar amount of arms
transfers to Taiwan might increase in the future. Finally, when
questioned by members of the press about the meaning of the
communiqué and its effect upon future arms sales to Taiwan,
President Reagan responded that "we're doing all the things that
we have always done. The shipments are regularly going
on. . . . Our Taiwan friends are going to continue to get
everything they need for their own self-defense."[22]

CONCLUSION

American policy toward the security of Taiwan is ambiguous.
For example, the TRA calls for a "peaceful resolution" of the
Taiwan issue and warns that the US would consider any hostile
actions directed against the ROC as "a threat to the peace and
security of the Western Pacific area and of grave concern to the
United States." But Washington is not committed to Taiwan's
defense. Furthermore, in the 1982 US-PRC Joint Communiqué,
the United States pledged to reduce its arms sales to the ROC
gradually, but it did not claim that such a reduction would be
readily apparent to an observer. The Reagan administration
conceded that the value of arms sales could actually rise in the
future, only to decline at a later date. Moreover, the United
States pledged to terminate arms sales to the ROC eventually, but
it gave no indication as to when this might happen.
    Interestingly, the ambiguity associated with the current
American position toward the security of Taiwan is not a radical
departure from past policy. When negotiating the terms of the
1954 US-ROC Mutual Defense Treaty, US officials were
concerned lest America be dragged into a war over the defense of

Taiwan's offshore islands. Consequently, John Foster Dulles, then US Secretary of State, suggested to the National Security Council that "it might be desirable . . . to 'fuzz up' to some extent the US reaction with regard to a Chinese Communist attack on Formosa [Taiwan] as such an attack would affect the Nationalist-held offshore islands."[23] Acting on Dulles' advice, the wording in Article V of the treaty was changed from "each party recognizes that an armed attack in the West Pacific Area *directed on* the territories of either of the Parties would be dangerous to its own peace and security" to "each party recognizes that an armed attack in the West Pacific *directed against* the territories of either of the Parties would be dangerous to its own peace and security." This seemingly minor change in language provided the US with some flexibility in determining how it would respond to PRC aggression. In this respect, one could argue that the current US ambiguous position toward the security of Taiwan is in keeping with long-standing policy.

While it is correct to assume that American policy toward the security of Taiwan gives all interested parties cause to complain, it is also correct to observe that the fluid nature of the policy contains something acceptable to all of the interested parties. The policy affords every interested party the luxury of being able to avoid losing face over the issue. For example, the PRC leadership may point with pride to the fact that the United States is no longer committed to Taiwan's defense and that it has finally agreed to reduce and eventually terminate arms sales to the ROC. In that respect, the current leadership in Beijing has succeeded where past leadership failed to persuade the US to stop meddling in China's internal affairs. On the other hand, authorities in Taipei may take solace in the fact that the United States has concluded a "tacit alliance" with the ROC and that it is going to continue to sell weapons to the ROC as mandated by the TRA. The flexibility of the policy also places American decisionmakers in the advantageous position of being able to establish a linkage between events in East Asia and America's commitment to the security of Taiwan. In this respect, the United States is able to

gain additional leverage in its relations with both Beijing and Taipei.
America's security relationship with Taiwan continues to be guided by the TRA and the 1982 US-PRC Joint Communiqué. The next two chapters show how the current policy has enabled Washington to provide Taipei with the technology and technological assistance necessary to produce its own weapons and, more recently, to sell sophisticated warplanes to Taiwan.

Notes

1. See *Taiwan Communiqué and Separation of Powers*, Report on the Taiwan Relations Act and the Joint Communique signed by the United States and China to the Committee On The Judiciary, United States Senate, Made by Its Subcommittee On Separation of Powers: Part One (Washington, D.C.: US Government Printing Office, 1983), p. 2.

2. According to members of Congress, a major failing in the Carter administration's version was that "it made no provision for American policy with regard to the future security of Taiwan." For more information, see J. Terry Emerson, "What Determines US Relations with China: The Taiwan Relations Act Or The August 17 Communiqué with Beijing," *Asian Studies Center Backgrounder*, November 30, 1987, p. 10.

3. Interestingly, Lai To Lee argues that the TRA went further than the Mutual Defense Treaty by "extending coverage to protect Taiwan from boycotts and embargoes not mentioned in the treaty." See Lai To Lee, *The Reunification of China: PRC-Taiwan Relations in Flux* (New York: Praeger Publishers, 1991), p. 62. However, because the TRA does not guarantee a US response to a hostile act, I do not agree with Lee's position. For a complete text of the act, see Appendix 1.

4. *United States-Taiwan Relations Act*, US House of Representatives, Committee on Foreign Affairs, 96th Congress, 1st Session, Report No. 96-26, 1979, p. 6.

5. *World Military Expenditures and Arms Transfers 1972-1982* (Washington, D.C.: US Arms Control and Disarmament Agency, 1984), p. 64.

6. For more information on US policy toward the future of Taiwan, see Dennis Van Vranken Hickey, "America's Two-Point Policy and the Future of Taiwan," Asian Survey 28, no. 8 (August 1988): 881-896.

7. "US Denies Relations Act Comments," *China Post* (International Airmail Edition), October 29, 1991, p. 1.

8. See "Campaign Statement by Ronald Reagan on US Policy Toward Asia and the Pacific, August 25, 1980, Los Angeles, California," in Appendix to Robert L. Downen, *Of Grave Concern: US-Taiwan Relations on the Threshold of the 1980's* (Washington, D.C.: Georgetown University, Center for Strategic and International Studies, 1981), p. 61.

9. For more information, see Alexander M. Haig, Jr., *Caveat: Realism, Reagan and Foreign Policy* (New York: Macmillan, 1984), pp. 194-214.

10. See Michel Oksenberg, "A Decade of Sino-American Relations," *Foreign Affairs* 61, no. 1 (Fall 1982): 191.

11. "No Sale of Advanced Aircraft to Taiwan," *Department of State Bulletin* no. 2059 (February 1982): 39.

12. *Taiwan Communiqué and Separation of Powers*, Hearing before the Subcommittee on Separation of Powers of the Committee of the Judiciary, United States Senate, 98th Congress, 1st Session on the Taiwan Relations Act and the Joint Communiqué signed by the United States and Peking: Part II, 1982), p. 23.

13. *Public Papers of the Presidents of the United States: Jimmy Carter, 1979,* Book I (Washington, D.C.: US Government Printing Office, 1980), p. 257.

14. Ibid.

15. See statement of Representative Mark D. Siljander (Republican-Michigan), in US House of Representatives, *Implementation of the Taiwan Relations Act*, Hearing and Markup before the Committee on Foreign Affairs and Its Subcommittee on Human Rights and International Organizations and on Asian and Pacific Affairs, p. 42.

16. *Public Papers of the Presidents of the United States: Ronald Reagan, 1983,* Book II, (Washington, D.C.: US Government Printing Office, 1985), p. 1646.

17. See Daniel Metraux, *Taiwan's Political and Economic Growth in The Late Twentieth Century* (Lewiston, New York: Edwin Mellen Press, 1991), p. 116.

18. "ROC Going to School on Gulf War Experiences, Defense Chief Says," *Free China Journal*, March 14, 1991, p. 2.

19. For an interesting discussion of the Six Assurances, see Martin L. Lasater, "US Arms Sales to Taiwan," in Steven W. Mosher (ed.), *The United States and the Republic of China: Democratic Friends, Strategic Allies and Economic Partners* (New Brunswick, New Jersey: Transaction Periodicals, 1992), p. 107.

20. See testimony of John H. Holdridge, Assistant Secretary, Bureau of East Asian and Pacific Affairs, Department of State, in *China and Taiwan*, Hearing Before the Committee on Foreign Relations, United States Senate, 97th Congress, 2d Session, August 17, 1982, p. 13.

21. Ibid. p. 23.

22. See "Interview with President Reagan," in Appendix, "Additional Submissions for the Record," *Taiwan Communiqué and the Separation of Powers*, p. 29.

23. See "Memorandum of Discussion at the 221st Meeting of the National Security Council, Washington, November 2, 1954," in *US Department of State, Foreign Relations of the United States 1952–1954*, vol. 14, pt. I (Washington, D.C.: US Government Printing Office, 1985), p. 829.

4

American Technological Assistance, Technology Transfers and Taiwan's Drive for Defense Self-Sufficiency

On October 10, 1991, the Republic of China celebrated its eightieth National Day with an impressive military parade, the sixteenth since the central government retreated to Taiwan in 1949. This event, the most massive military parade ever arranged in Taiwan's history, was televised live on each of the island's three television stations and afforded the government an excellent opportunity to showcase its martial prowess. What distinguished this parade from past displays of military hardware, however, was the surprisingly large array of domestically manufactured aircraft, air-defense missiles, anti-submarine helicopters, tanks, jeeps, and other implements of war.

Caspar Weinberger, former US Secretary of Defense, has described Taiwan's recent progress in arms development as "remarkable."[1] This chapter examines America's support of Taiwan's drive for defense self-sufficiency. It outlines American policy on Taiwan's arms development, explores recent progress in its weapons research and development program and discusses potential benefits and liabilities that such a program may pose for the United States.

AMERICAN POLICY

America's policy on military assistance to Taiwan is principally outlined in the TRA and the 1982 US-PRC Communiqué. According to the TRA, US policy is to "make available to Taiwan such defense articles and defense services in such quantity as may be necessary to enable Taiwan to maintain a sufficient self-defense capability."[2] However, according to the 1982 Communiqué:

> The U.S. government states that it does not seek to carry out a long term policy of arms sales to Taiwan and will not exceed, either in qualitative or quantitative terms, the level of those supplied in recent years since the establishment of diplomatic relations between the United States and China, and that it intends to reduce gradually its sales of arms to Taiwan, leading over a period of time to a final resolution.[3]

Since the early 1980s, the PRC has sought relentlessly to modernize its military. Although these efforts may not be motivated by a great desire to threaten Taiwan, they have undermined the defensive capabilities of Taiwan vis-a-vis the PRC nevertheless. Given this state of affairs, the United States confronts a predicament. On the one hand, it is pledged to ensure that Taiwan maintains a sufficient self-defense capability. On the other hand, it seemed to promise in the 1982 communiqué that it would not exceed, in either qualitative or quantitative terms, the level of arms supplied during the early 1980s and to reduce gradually its sales of arms to Taiwan. In order to overcome these inconsistencies in policy, the United States has sought to capitalize on the ambiguities and loopholes to be found in the 1982 Communiqué.

Government-to-Government Arms Transfers

Under the Foreign Military Sales (FMS) program, "the US government essentially purchases equipment from manufacturers (or draws it from Department of Defense stocks) and resells it to foreign customers."[4] The second column in Table 4.1 outlines the value of direct American FMS transfers to Taiwan for fiscal years 1983 through 1991. The sales figures represent the value of contracts signed by the American Institute in Taipei (for the US) and the Coordination Council for North American Affairs (for Taiwan). It is clear that direct FMS transfers to Taiwan have dropped substantially.

Table 4.1
United States FMS Arms Agreements with Taiwan and Commercial Arms Exports to Taiwan: FY 1983–1991 (Thousands of U.S. Dollars)

FY	FMS	Commercial	Total
1983	689.0	5.0	774.0
1984	707.4	70.0	777.4
1985	700.2	54.5	754.7
1986	510.8	228.0	738.8
1987	509.0	210.0	719.0
1988	505.0	195.0	700.0
1989	526.3	4.7	611.0
1990	509.0	149.9	658.9
1991	480.0	160.0	640.0

Source: Defense Security Assistance Agency, *Foreign Military Sales, Foreign Military Construction Sales and Military Assistance Facts As of September 30, 1991* (Washington, D.C.: Data Management Division, Comptroller, DSAA, 1991).

Commercial Arms Sales

In commercial arms transfers, American companies sell directly to foreign governments. Such sales must be approved by the Department of State's Office of Munitions Control. The third column in Table 4.1 outlines the value of privately exported American arms to Taiwan (commercial arms agreements) for fiscal years 1983 through 1991. These sales figures, which are based on US customs receipts, receive less publicity and public scrutiny than FMS transfers. As the value of direct American FMS exports to Taiwan has decreased, the value of military items which Taiwan has been able to purchase through licensed commercial channels has grown substantially. Despite this rise, however, the total value of all American arms transfers to Taiwan has continued to decline. As outlined in the fourth column in Table 4.1, combined FMS and commercial agreements between the two countries—valued at approximately $774 million in FY 1983—had dropped to $640 million in FY 1991.

Technological Assistance and Technology Transfers

America's policy of providing Taiwan with the technology and technological assistance necessary to produce its own weapons might be traced to President Richard M. Nixon's call in 1969 for a world-wide reduction of American forces overseas (the Nixon Doctrine). One of the principal elements of the doctrine was the liberalization of America's military technology export codes, so that countries such as Taiwan "were afforded far greater access to sophisticated US technology than had ever before been the case."[5] The decision to seek a rapprochement with Beijing furthered this policy, which would enable the US to reduce its military presence on the island.

Beginning in the late 1960s, the US assisted Taiwan with a number of projects designed to help it establish a fledgling defense industry. Taiwan rapidly developed a capability to manufacture small arms, ammunition and artillery pieces. Perhaps most notable during this period was the 1973 agreement between the Northrop Corporation and Taiwan to co-produce Northrop's F-5E/F fighter aircraft. This project helped to lay the groundwork for Taiwan's avionics industry.

During the years following the issuance of the 1982 US-PRC Joint Communiqué, American technological assistance and technology transfers to Taiwan increased markedly. The US adopted the position that the restrictions of the communiqué do not cover American technological assistance or the transfer of American technology to Taiwan. This viewpoint enabled the US to overcome what might otherwise be considered irreconcilable contradictions in policy. It allowed Washington both to "reduce gradually its sales of arms to Taiwan" (observing the provisions of the communiqué), and to ensure that Taiwan "maintains a sufficient self-defense capability" (complying with the provisions of the TRA). US officials defended this narrow interpretation by arguing that "the text [of the communiqué] is clear. . . . It talks of arms sales and not technology."[6]

Everything from computer chips to helicopters may fall under the broad rubric of "technological assistance," "dual-use technology" or "technology transfer." For this reason and because some US-assisted projects have remained classified, the nature and value of American technological assistance is most difficult to calculate. US Department of Commerce (DOC) data, however, may provide a rough approximation of the growth in such transfers.

According to the terms of the Export Administration Act of 1979, the DOC and Department of Defense (DOD) are charged with the responsibility of exercising control over the export of strategic commodities and technologies. These departments maintain a list of critical commodities and technologies with military applications, commonly referred to as the Commodity Control List (CCL). In order to export a CCL item, an American corporation must obtain a license from the DOC.

Table 4.2 outlines the value of Taiwan CCL export licenses granted for the years 1985 through mid-1989.

Table 4.2
Approved CCL Applications to Taiwan, 1985-1989 (Thousands of U.S. Dollars)

	1985	1986	1987	1988	1/89-6/89
VALUE	197,278	1,986,723	6,435,740	10,815,152	3,814,913

Source: Data provided courtesy of the Export Administration, U.S. Department of Commerce, Washington, D.C. Note: value of licenses approved does not reflect value of actual licensed shipments which may be substantially less.

Table 4.3
Value of CCL Licenses for Selected Commodities, 1985-1989 (Thousands of U.S. Dollars)

	1985	1986	1987	1988	1/89-6/8
Electronic Assemblies & Integrated Circuits	37,669	736,267	3,963,625	4,854,015	2,142,408
Computing Equipment, Electronic	104,853	782,876	1,736,003	5,324,034	1,178,603
Semiconductor Diodes (Specified)	4,332	17,584	22,749	57,836	5,723

Source: Data provided courtesy of the Export Administration, U.S. Department of Commerce, Washington, D.C. Note: value of licenses approved does not reflect value of actual licensed shipments, which may be substantially less.

During the 1980s, the value of American dual-use technology exports to Taiwan began to grow significantly. Electronic machinery exports, especially computing equipment, electronics assemblies and integrated circuits, have been areas of particularly strong growth. Table 4.3 outlines the growth in the value of CCL licenses for selected dual-use commodities between 1985 and June 1989. Since that time, the value of American dual-use technology exports has continued to rise. DOC statistics reveal that "applications approved for Taiwan during the period January 1, 1988 through December 31, 1991 totaled 11,601, representing 221 commodity control numbers and the total dollar value was $23,439,176,150."[7]

Most often, official sources in Washington and Taipei have refused to comment upon American technology transfers to Taiwan.[8] For example, when questioned by the press in 1988, Weinberger claimed that he was not aware of any "particular American participation or transfer of technology" intended to upgrade Taiwan's weapons systems.[9] In November of that same year, however, Cheng Wei-yuan, Taiwan's Defense Minister, confirmed what many had long suspected when he admitted that his nation's new fighter aircraft, tanks and guided missile frigates are "being developed with technology provided by the US."[10]

RECENT PROGRESS IN TAIWAN'S DRIVE FOR DEFENSE SELF-SUFFICIENCY

By the early 1980s, much of Taiwan's military arsenal was approaching obsolescence. Even more worrisome for Taiwan, the United States and numerous other arms-exporting nations had opted to reduce or terminate their arms sales to Taiwan rather than risk reprisals from Beijing. The 1982 American decision not to sell Taiwan a sophisticated warplane, designated the FX fighter by the Pentagon, was an especially bitter pill for Taipei. At the same time, the PRC was rapidly expanding its military capabilities. In order to maintain a credible deterrent against a possible PRC attack or, more likely, a naval blockade, Taiwan's military would have to modernize. Two factors intervened at this point to rescue Taiwan from its desperate plight. First, the US adopted the position that the restrictions of the 1982 US-PRC Joint Communiqué did not cover American technological assistance or the transfer of American technology to Taiwan. Additionally, with its foreign exchange reserves climbing to astronomical proportions for a country of its size (topping over US $87 billion), Taiwan could well afford to import technology, commit extensive funds to weapons research and development programs and purchase any arms it could from the United States and other nations.

Armed with American technological assistance and its hard currency reserves, Taiwan has launched an impressive drive aimed at military modernization and defense self-sufficiency. The overall objective of this campaign is to retain control of the Taiwan Strait, the surrounding sea-lanes and its territorial airspace, while maintaining an ability to repulse an amphibious assault. In order to realize these goals, numerous ventures are underway. The following discussion explores the development of four of Taiwan's more ambitious projects: an advanced fighter aircraft; a range of sophisticated missiles; a second generation of warships and an upgraded main battle tank.

Indigenous Defense Fighter

Development of Taiwan's Indigenous Defense Fighter (IDF), also known as the Chiang Ching-kuo fighter, began in 1982 at the instruction of the late President Chiang Ching-kuo because of the government's difficulty in purchasing fighter aircraft from abroad.[11] Defense Minister Chen Li-an later explained, "We had the money, but nowhere to buy the aircraft."[12] Making matters worse, Taipei began to experience difficulties obtaining spare parts for its warplanes.[13]

The IDF was developed by the Aero Industry Development Center (AIDC), a subsidiary of Taiwan's primary defense-related research and development facility, the Chung Shan Institute of Science and Technology (CSIST). The new warplane was unveiled officially on December 12, 1988, and military officials announced that it would eventually replace Taiwan's aging stock of more than 80 Lockheed F-104G and 300 plus Northrop F-5E/F aircraft. Estimates of the total cost of the aircraft's research and production budget vary. In 1988, sources in Taipei estimated that "the budget for development and production of the fighter runs up to US \$1 billion."[14] By 1990, the budget for developing the fighter had climbed to US \$2.2 billion.[15] Still other sources have placed the total cost much higher.

Several American corporations have reportedly provided the AIDC with technological assistance for the project. According to *Jane's Defence Weekly*:

General Dynamics acted as consultant for the airframe, after initially providing technical specifications and drawings from its F-16 programme. . . . The engine was developed by Garrett . . . [and] Lear Siegler has integrated the avionics package.[16]

However, Taiwan authorities stress that each stage of the warplane's development was chiefly handled by Taiwan.

The IDF's performance characteristics are still top secret. But *Jane's* has reported that its two TFE1042 engines, each of which has approximately 8,500 pounds of static thrust with afterburner, "should produce a speed in excess of Mach 1.2 . . . [and] further development aims to achieve 12,000 lb of thrust with afterburner to produce a speed of Mach 1.6–1.8 in later models."[17] The warplane is also equipped with an advanced fly-by-wire operating system that increases its maneuverability. Colonel Wu Kang-ming, an IDF test pilot, observed, "It does whatever you want."[18]

Armed with its domestically manufactured air-to-air and/or anti-ship missiles and a General Electric Vulcan M-61A cannon (capable of firing 100 rounds per second), the aircraft is expected to serve as an air superiority fighter with anti-ship capabilities. By late 1991, four prototypes of the warplane had been developed, and the first assembly-line IDF is scheduled to join Taiwan's air force sometime in 1992 or 1993.[19] Taipei had planned originally to manufacture over 250 IDFs. Following the acquisition of advanced American and French fighters in 1992, however, the military reduced its order to 135 planes.[20]

During the initial stages of the IDF project, authorities on Taiwan were pleased with its prospects. In 1988, military specialists boasted confidently that "the development of the fighter will allow Taipei to maintain air superiority over the Taiwan Strait in the 1990s."[21] Spin-off benefits were anticipated as well. President Lee Teng-hui claimed that the fighter demonstrated visibly that Taiwan was now at "a starting point to advance into the high technology aeronautics industry."[22] Hau Pei-tsun, then Chief of the General Staff, concurred with the President's opinion and described the aircraft as "a military breakthrough" that would have important "spin-off benefits for other areas of technology."[23]

The Bush administration's September 2, 1992, decision to sell 150 F-16/A and F-16/B fighters to Taiwan may have placed some aspects of the multi-billion-dollar IDF program in doubt. Two days after the Bush announcement, Taiwan's state-funded Central News Agency reported that the government had scrapped plans to upgrade and improve the IDF. The Defense Ministry, however, quickly denied the report:

The report about our terminating the program to improve and upgrade the performance of the Ching Kuo IDF warplanes is groundless. Our improvement program will be carried out according to the set schedule and we have no plan to stop it.[24]

It is unclear how the F-16 sale will affect the IDF program. But US officials stress that major technology transfers will not accompany the sale.[25]

Missile Development Program

Taiwan is producing advanced versions of several domestically manufactured missiles. In addition to the development of a surface-to-surface missile (SSM), the CSIST has developed at least two varieties of surface-to-air missiles (SAMs), air-to-air missiles (AAMs) and anti-ship missiles. The government hopes to become self-sufficient in such weapons.

Taiwan's SSM, the Ching Feng (Green Bee), made its debut during the 1981 National Day military parade. It is a medium-range missile with a maximum range of over 100 kilometers. The Ching Feng was reportedly developed with Israeli assistance, and its "nearest likely relative is the American Lance battlefield support weapon."[26] Capable of delivering either a conventional or a nuclear warhead, production is believed to have ceased under pressure from the United States. Plans for a proposed Ching Feng-II, with a range of 1,000 kilometers, appear also to have been scrapped.

Taiwan's SAMs, the Tien Kung-I and Tien Kung-II (Sky Bow-I and Sky Bow-II), or collectively the Chungcheng 100 series, will be incorporated into a sophisticated air defense network that the government hopes to deploy by the mid-1990s. Military officials believe that this system will make Beijing think twice before launching an air attack against Taiwan. Dr. Chen Li-an, Taiwan's Defense Minister, explains: "Should a war take place, the ROC's forces will be able to put up a strong defense by intercepting enemy attacks with the help of missiles."[27]

Taiwan's Tien Kung-I is a low to medium-altitude SAM with an estimated range of 30 to 40 kilometers. The weapon has been described as "a hybrid of the US-made Patriot (dimensions and launcher) and the US-made Hawk (electronics) with performance characteristics midway between the two."[28] The new Tien Kung-II, which was first viewed publicly during the October 1988 National Day parade, is a high-altitude SAM with a projected range of 100 kilometers. It has been described as being "derived from the US-made Nike Hercules, which it will replace in Taiwan's arsenal."[29]   In August 1989, the first set of Tien Kung missiles was completed and delivered to the ROC Army for tests and training.[30] Currently, improvements are being made.   Taiwan's SAM program received a major boost in December 1991 when the Bush administration quietly authorized the sale of key radar, guidance and command-control components of the Patriot missile to Taiwan.[31]   It received another boost in September 1992 when the US agreed to sell the Patriot missile system to Taiwan.   Under the terms of this $1.1 billion agreement, US-based Raytheon and Taipei will co-produce a Patriot missile derivative.   According to the US Department of State:

> Raytheon will provide the missile forebody, ground support equipment, training, maintenance and technical support. Taiwan will produce the aft section of the missile, which will include the warhead assembly, propulsion and control sections, in accordance with a Raytheon technical data package.[32]

Notice of the missile coproduction deal reached Congress shortly after President Bush announced his intention to sell 150 F-16/A and F-16/B warplanes to Taiwan.

In addition to the SAM program, the CSIST has developed two new indigenous AAMs: the Tien Chien–I and Tien Chien–II (Sky Sword–I and Sky Sword–II). These missiles are expected to help Taiwan retain control of its territorial airspace. The existence of the Tien Chien–I was first revealed in 1986. It is a short range (10 to 15 kilometers) homing missile "bearing a close external resemblance to the US built Sidewinder."[33]   As of 1991, the Tien Chien–I had undergone over 1,400 hours of testing.[34]   The Tien Chien–II is reportedly a medium-range version of the Tien Chien–I. Both types of missiles will be carried by the new IDF aircraft and "have excellent computerized guidance systems that stand up to the most advanced counter electronics."[35] Furthermore, Taiwan's cabinet has revealed that the Defense Ministry "has also produced land and sea based versions of the Tien Chien to make Tien Chien Missiles useful in all three branches of the military."[36]

The CSIST has developed two anti-ship missiles, the Hsiung Feng-I and Hsiung Feng-II (Awe-inspiring Air I and II). The Hsiung Feng-I is "a license-built Taiwanese version of the Israeli Gabriel anti-ship missile."[37] A formidable sea-skimming anti-ship missile, the weapon has an estimated range of 30 to 40 kilometers. After several years of testing, the military has deployed both ground and sea-borne versions of the Hsiung Feng-I. When deployed at sea, the missiles are fitted aboard destroyers of the US Gearing and Allen M. Summer classes or aboard indigenously developed fast attack craft and missile frigates. Ashore, the missiles are only one component in a sophisticated mobile defense system that is thought to have been constructed with American technological assistance.

The Hsiung Feng-II, which made its first public appearance at the 1988 National Day parade, is a longer-range (80 kilometers or more) version of the Hsiung Feng-I. In 1991, the Defense Ministry announced that "mass production" of the Hsiung Feng-II "is in full swing."[38] The CSIST is also studying the feasibility of an air-deployed model of the Hsiung Feng.

A Second Generation of Warships

With over 180 vessels of varying sizes and over 200,000 tons of displacement, Taiwan's navy is one of the ten largest navies in the world.[39] In terms of larger vessels, Taiwan currently deploys 24 destroyers—a mix of Gearing, Summer and Fletcher-class ships built by the US—as well as nine frigates.[40] Built in the 1940s, most of these vessels are approaching obsolescence. Admiral Yeh Chang-tung, Taiwan's navy commander-in-chief, has acknowledged that "today they average over 45 years in service, and are almost at the stage where they are too old to use."[41]

In order to retain control of the surrounding sea-lanes, Taiwan must modernize its Navy.   Consequently, it is manufacturing several varieties of missile-equipped fast-attack craft, refurbishing its World War II-era destroyers and developing plans to build a submarine. Its most ambitious naval construction project to date, however, is the Kuanghua-I project—the development of a second generation of warships.

In 1987, "the U.S. quietly sold Taiwan blueprints and data packages necessary to build FFG-Oliver Hazard Perry-class frigates, similar to the USS Stark attacked in the Persian Gulf."[42] With Bath Iron Works of the United States providing technical assistance, Taiwan's China Shipbuilding Corporation is constructing at least eight 3,600-ton Perry-class frigates. When completed, the warships will carry the new Hsiung Feng-II missile and reportedly possess formidable anti-aircraft, anti-ship and anti-submarine capabilities:

Main antiaircraft weaponry is a single MK-13 missile launcher at the bows, and the improved Harpoon anti-ship missile launcher can fire standard antiaircraft missiles.   The ship carries two S-70C helicopters, known for superb antisubmarine capability, in addition to the ASROC antisubmarine rocket and the MK-46 pursuit missile, well suited for search and detection during shallow water warfare. The ship also has 76mm rapid artillery, the MK-16 multiple cannon, 40mm rapid artillery and the domestically produced Hsiung Feng-2 missile, giving it formidable overall firepower.[43]

The lead frigate was completed in January 1990 and a second in October 1992. After undergoing extensive testing, the first frigate (the Cheng Kung-1011), was formally commissioned on May 7, 1993.[44] The remaining ships will be completed at the rate of roughly one every 11 months.

Upgraded Main Battle Tanks

In order to maintain its ability to repulse an amphibious invasion, Taiwan began over a decade ago to upgrade its nearly obsolete M48A1 main battle tanks (MBT). Over 300 MBTs are now believed to have attained the much-improved M48A5 standards.[45] As opposed to the M48A1, the M48A5 is powered by a new diesel-driven engine (produced by US-based Teledyne Continental Motors) and fitted with modern thermal imaging and fire control systems. Fire power has also increased with the installation of a 105-mm gun.

Taiwan has also developed a new and lighter version of the American M60 MBT—the M48H or "Brave Tiger". During 1984–85, General Dynamics' Land Systems Division was awarded over US $33 million in contracts for approximately 215 ready-to-assemble M60A bodies. The company reportedly received another order valued at over US $39 million in 1986.[46] The new MBTs are equipped with a laser rangefinder, infrared night vision system, ballistic computer and improved armor protection. It is capable of traveling at a top speed of 30 miles per hour and can traverse bodies of water up to 8 feet deep.

On April 14, 1990, the first domestically developed M48H tank was unveiled officially during a public demonstration held at Taiwan's Armor Research and Development Center. During the christening ceremony, Minister of Defense Hau Pei-tsun declared that "this is one of the finest moments in the Army's history. . . . Production of the M48 is one of the greatest achievements of the 65 year-old force."[47] Since that time, over 150 Brave Tigers have been manufactured. Taiwan plans to produce over 400 more.[48]

Summary

Each of the projects described is designed to play a crucial role in the military's operational defense strategy, code-named Ku

An (Solid Peace).[49] Current tactics call for an invasion force to confront seven lines of defense. The island's foremost defensive arc consists of its potent missile forces. The final line of defense consists of the army and its MBT forces. In the event that an invader does manage to land on the island, the army is not expected to drive it from the beaches. Rather, existing plans call for the military to "make its principal stand with its tanks and best troops along the highways, making use of these communications lines to concentrate forces against the invading army's main attack axes."[50] The overall goal of the strategy, however, is to destroy an invasion force before it reaches the island. In order to accomplish this task, Taiwan will not hesitate to take the war to the mainland. The current battle plan "calls for immediately knocking out all radar stations along the mainland's southeast coast, as well as the 13 Communist airbases within 250 nautical miles of Taiwan."[51]

This discussion outlined only the development of four of Taiwan's most ambitious defense projects. A more complete description would contain details of other enterprises as well. Taiwan has never stopped research on nuclear arms development. According to Yen Chen-hsing, chairman of Taiwan's Atomic Energy Council, Taiwan "absolutely" has the capability to manufacture nuclear weapons.[52] Moreover, in 1990 one ROC government ministry official inadvertently reported that CSIST "is involved in making atomic bombs."[53] Additional ventures include the recent development of the Kun Wu anti-tank missile, Kung Feng III/IV multiple rocket system, Working Bee-6 artillery rocket, Tien Kung radar and T-34 jet trainer.

A more complete accounting would also explore recent defensive measures that have been undertaken in order to secure military personnel, equipment, and facilities from surprise attack. In July 1988, General Liu Chih-chung, Assistant Chief of the military's General Planning Staff, revealed that the Defense Ministry "has moved the nation's key military installations underground in an effort to prevent missile attacks from Communist China."[54] This multi-billion-dollar project, code-named Chia Shan, includes underground shelters for fighter aircraft and submarine facilities (it was completed in late 1991). The General also announced that "major military bases" have been relocated to Taiwan's east coast, which is shielded from the PRC by the Central Mountain range, and that Taiwan plans to "counter Communist Chinese missile attacks with its own anti-missile shell."[55]

As part of its defensive strategy, Defense Minister Chen Li-an has revealed that Taiwan is stepping up its intelligence gathering operations on the mainland. Most of these activities are concentrated in the PRC's Nanjing military region—the military zone directly across the strait from Taiwan and reportedly designated as the staging area for any PRC invasion of the island.[56] According to Taiwan estimates, Beijing has deployed three army groups—consisting of 320,000 troops, 1,600 tanks and six reserve divisions—in the area.[57]

Finally, it is noteworthy that Taiwan is attempting to secure military equipment, hardware and technology from sources other than the United States. For example, in October 1991, as part of its naval modernization program, Taiwan successfully negotiated the purchase of 16 La Fayette–class frigates from France. Under the terms of the arrangement, the first six hulls will be built in France and delivered to Taiwan in sections for assembly in 1994. The remainder will be constructed in Taiwan with the assistance of France's state-run firm, Thomson-CSF.[58] In December 1992, this agreement was followed with a deal for 60 French-made Mirage 2000-5 warplanes.

TAIWAN'S DRIVE FOR DEFENSE SELF-SUFFICIENCY: POTENTIAL RISKS TO AMERICAN SECURITY INTERESTS

American technological assistance and a plentiful supply of hard currency have enabled Taiwan to make impressive strides in its crusade for defense self-sufficiency. This campaign, however, presents potential risks to American security interests.

An Issue in US-PRC Relations

From the PRC's perspective, it is the American government, not Taiwan, that stands in the way of a peaceful reunification of China. PRC officials have long insisted that the steady supply of American arms creates a climate encouraging the Taiwan authorities not to enter into reunification negotiations. They see little difference between supplying Taiwan directly with arms and supplying Taiwan with the technology necessary to manufacture arms.

In 1986, the Chinese Communist Party General Secretary Hu Yaobang was asked to comment upon the American position that the 1982 US-PRC Joint Communiqué does not cover the transfer of technology to Taiwan. According to Hu:

It [technology transfer] is not mentioned directly, but it is clearly covered. What is the difference between arms sales and the transfer of technology for the manufacture of armament? "Transfer of technology" sounds better, but it is the same thing as arms sales.[59]

Hu described the American stance on this issue as the most "serious problem" in Sino-American relations and warned that "if it is a fact that the US is using technology transfers to circumvent the limits on quantitative and qualitative increases, it would constitute bad faith. . . . China would take a stern position and would give serious consideration to the proper measures of response."[60] Other PRC officials went further and accused the American government of being "drunk" with its power.[61]

China's position toward this matter has not softened. Reacting to Washington's January 1992 decision to provide Taiwan with advanced Patriot missile technology, the PRC charged that the sale violates agreements between Washington and Beijing.

According to Wu Jianmin, a PRC Foreign Ministry spokesman, Beijing is "seriously concerned about the matter" and "firmly opposed to *any action* of the United States to upgrade the level of performance of the weapons it sells to Taiwan [emphasis added]."[62] In sum, American policy holds the potential to strain US-PRC relations.

Taiwan as a Technology Exporter

Owing largely to the peculiarities of the current "unofficial" state of US-Taiwan relations, no formal mechanism exists to prevent Taiwan from channeling sensitive American technology to other countries. The US and Taiwan have not signed a bilateral high-technology agreement, and Taiwan was never invited to join the Coordinating Committee on Multilateral Export Control (COCOM), an organization of North American Treaty Organization (NATO) countries and Japan that sought to harmonize export controls to Soviet-bloc nations. As Taiwan continues to acquire sophisticated American technology, while simultaneously expanding its trade relations throughout the world, the risk of sensitive American technology finding its way into the hands of irresponsible Third World dictators could rise.

There is also a danger that advanced American technology may fall into the hands of the PRC. Indeed, some have suggested that the 1982 rejection of Taiwan's request to purchase advanced fighter aircraft "was in part due to the US fears that the PRC might gain technological intelligence from aircraft subsequently captured from the ROC [Taiwan]."[63]

Taiwan as an Arms Exporter

As Taiwan increases its ability to manufacture a variety of sophisticated weapons, it might be tempted to follow the lead of numerous other governments and market its arms. Taiwan officials have boasted that a foreign aerospace expert told the ROC's Paris Air Show representatives that "if the IDF were exhibited here, 40 or 50 would be sold the very first day, I guarantee you."[64] *Aviation Week and Space Technology* concurs with this assessment. Noting that the IDF "probably will be one of the few new-technology, lightweight, twin-engine fighters in production in the mid-1990s," the journal speculated that the warplane "has long-term export potential."[65]

Taiwan exports only a small amount of arms (Table 4.4), and exporting highly advanced weaponry is against ROC government policy. However, the potential benefits of such a policy may prove too much to resist. An aggressive arms-exporting program could enable Taiwan both to generate enough hard currency to pay for many of its own arms imports and bolster political ties with arms-purchasing countries. If one employs Taiwan's past arms sales as an indicator, there is reason to believe that such a program may undermine American interests.

Table 4.4
Taiwan's Arms Exports, 1981–1989 (Constant 1989 Millions of U.S. Dollars)

1981	1982	1983	1984	1985	1986	1987	1988	1989
54	0	6	12	6	6	11	21	10

Source: US Arms Control and Disarmament Agency, *World Military Expenditures and Arms Transfers, 1990* (Washington, D.C.: US Government Printing Office, 1992), p. 100.

Taiwan exports a large percentage of its arms to governments in Latin America. Most of these arms have been accurately described as clones of American-designed weaponry—the very weapons utilized by most Latin American governments. With similar engineering, operation and sometimes even interchangeable parts, these weapons often complement, rather than conflict with, an existing United States–equipped military arsenal. When the United States has deemed it appropriate to reduce or terminate its arms sales, Taiwan has not hesitated to step in and fill the void:

> Earlier this year [1988] Congress blocked an appropriation of M16 rifles for the Salvadoran police forces because of human rights abuses. However a shipment of Taiwanese Type 65 rifles arrived in El Salvador in June. A similar shipment of Type 65s also arrived this summer in Panama; the Panamanian Defense Forces are under a total arms embargo from the USA.[66]

Taiwan has also exported arms to other world regions. During the 1990–1991 Persian Gulf War, reports circulated that Taipei had helped Iraq circumvent the allied-imposed trade embargo. According to these, Iraq obtained military equipment and materials used in the manufacture of poison gas from Taiwan and several other countries.[67] However, Dr. Shaw Yu-ming, then Director-General of the ROC Government Information Office, branded the stories "totally groundless."[68] Moreover, on March 20, 1991, Taiwan's Executive Yuan issued a statement saying that "there are no records of arms sales to Iraq" and that "the ROC policy is to sell arms only to friendly, non-communist countries in accordance with 'The Regulations Governing Military Export Operations'."[69] But disturbing reports about other weapons sales—including a mysterious arms deal between Taipei and Tehran—have also surfaced.[70]

During the Cold War, both the United States and the Soviet Union began to use arms sales as a means by which to wield influence in the Third World. Beginning in the 1960s, however, Soviet bargaining power started to suffer with the increasing availability of PRC clones of Soviet weaponry. American influence might similarly decline should Taiwan make available its copies of American weaponry.

If Taiwan should choose not to export its arms, there still exists a danger that Taipei might blackmail the US with its ability to produce and export advanced weaponry. As one authority observed, "A credible arms production capability of a certain degree of sophistication can be used both to threaten the design and production of weapons distasteful to the United States, so as to receive concessions for subsequently refraining from such production, and, when the threats cease to work as they should, actually to produce the weapons in question, for use or for export."[71]

Unrest on Taiwan

In 1981, two authorities on Taiwan's politics described a possible attempt by Taiwan to produce, domestically, the weapons necessary for its own defense as "an elaborate cost-inefficient employment of resources now committed to industrialization and modernization."[72] Furthermore, it was argued that such an effort would likely necessitate the adoption of austerity programs which would "invariably bring increased political control and population-management necessities."[73] This analysis was only partially in error.

Although Taiwan's push for defense self-sufficiency has not led to the adoption of austerity programs or resulted in increased political control, it is undoubtedly an elaborate cost-inefficient employment of the government's resources. Taipei would save billions of dollars in research and development funds if it was able to secure its aircraft, missiles and other sophisticated weaponry from abroad. Thus far, the government's enormous hard currency reserves have enabled it to invest substantial sums in defense-related projects without cutting back on social services. If government revenue should drop, however, all of this may change.

Table 4.5 outlines Taiwan's military budget and its percentage of GNP and central government expenditures for the years 1979 through 1989. Table 4.6 shows Taiwan's ranking among the world's leading arms recipients. These military expenditures have become an issue on the island. In April 1992, lawmakers slashed a record NT $3.6 billion from the military budget.[74] However, some members of the opposition Democratic Progressive Party (DPP) still charge that far too large a share of the national budget is committed to defense. The DPP disputes the government's claims that less than 30 percent of the national budget is allocated for military spending. It charges that the military's real share of the fiscal budget is much higher. If the government experienced a revenue shortfall and opted to reduce social spending rather than cut defense, thousands of those affected by such cuts might take to the streets. This situation could well lead to instability, violence and government repression. The ultimate outcome of such a scenario is difficult to predict, but almost certainly it would not be in the best interests of the United States.

TAIWAN'S DRIVE FOR DEFENSE SELF-SUFFICIENCY: POTENTIAL BENEFITS TO AMERICAN SECURITY INTERESTS

America's continued support of Taiwan's drive for defense self-sufficiency could jeopardize American security interests. At the same time, however, the policy might advance American foreign policy goals and objectives.

East Asian Peace and Stability

Although the PRC claims that it seeks a peaceful reunification of China, it has never ruled out the use of force. Beijing fluctuates in its calculations about invading or blockading Taiwan; if the cost is high, it may hesitate, but if the cost is low, it may decide that the benefits of such actions outweigh the costs.

Table 4.5

Taiwan's Military Expenditures, Percentage of GNP and Percentage of Central Government Expenditures, 1979-1989 (Constant 1989 Millions of U.S. Dollars)

YEAR	EXPENDITURES	% OF GNP	% OF CGE
1979	4539	6.6	29.9
1980	4748	6.5	28.0
1981	4962	6.4	NA
1982	6171	7.7	46.8
1983	6815	7.8	48.4
1984	6244	6.4	46.8
1985	7260E	7.0	50.0
1986	7535E	6.5	50.0
1987	5913E	4.6	41.5
1988	6877E	4.9	31.3
1989	8060E	5.4	30.3

Note: E equals US ACDA estimate; NA equals data not available.
Source: US Arms Control and Disarmament Agency, *World Military Expenditure and Arms Transfers, 1990* (Washington, D.C.:   US Government Printing Office, 1992), p. 58.

American authorities estimate that "the number of divisions required to invade Taiwan successfully range upward of 40 or more—roughly one-third of the People's Liberation Army."[75] According to official Taiwan government estimates, the island's defense forces are "capable of repelling a Chinese Communist attack of 2,000 jet fighters, 200 warships and 20 divisions simultaneously."[76]   A blockade, which would probably escalate quickly into conflict, would likewise prove an expensive move.

Thus far, the costs associated with any invasion or blockade attempt have caused PRC officials to conclude that such action is not feasible.   In May 1985, Hu Yaobang said that "everyone knows we have not yet the military power to attack Taiwan. . . . This temporary period may last four [to] eight years."[77]   More

Table 4.6
Arms Deliveries to Leading Third World Recipients, 1991
(1991 Millions of U.S. Dollars)

Rank	Recipient	Deliveries
1	Saudi Arabia	7,100
2	Afghanistan	1,900
3	Iran	1,500
4	India	800
5	Egypt	700
6	Syria	600
7	Cuba	500
8	Taiwan	500
9	Burma	300
10	Libya	300

Source: Richard Grimmett, Congressional Research Service, *Conventional Arms Transfers to the Third World, 1984-1991* (Washington, D.C.: Library of Congress, July 20, 1992, p. 72.

recently, in September 1988, Jen Pin-sheng, Deputy Director of Beijing's Taiwan Research Institute, admitted that "the Four Modernizations Program would not allow Peking to waste energy or money on a military takeover of Taiwan."[78] Cognizant of Beijing's calculations, ROC officials have revealed that a key element in Taiwan's defense strategy is "keeping a mainland invasion prohibitively costly in terms of casualities [and] materials.[79]

One of the primary objectives of America's East Asian policy is to maintain "regional peace, stability and prosperity."[80] Any hostile action directed against Taiwan would destabilize the region and undermine this goal. Taiwan's campaign for defense self-sufficiency ensures that the costs associated with any PRC invasion or blockade attempt will remain exorbitantly high and thereby increases the likelihood of continued regional harmony and development. As such, America's technological assistance and technology transfers to Taiwan promote American foreign policy objectives.

A Bargaining Chip in U.S.-China Relations

America's policy of assisting Taiwan in its drive for defense self-sufficiency enables the US to gain additional leverage in its relations with both the PRC and Taiwan. The flexibility of the policy allows the US to establish a linkage between the PRC's foreign policy behavior and the level of American technological assistance to Taiwan. For example, if the PRC chose to adopt a more threatening stance toward Taiwan, the level of technological assistance might increase. If, on the other hand, the PRC pledged not to use force to reunite China, the level of technological assistance could decrease.

The policy also provides the US with additional leverage in its relations with Taiwan. The US could use this leverage to obtain concessions on trade issues and/or encourage Taiwan's continued moves toward political liberalization.[81] It could also seek to establish a clear linkage between Taiwan's arms or technology exports to the Third World and its continued access to American technology.

China Policy Consensus

During the 1980s, important domestic political interests were served by America's continued support of Taiwan's drive for defense self-sufficiency. The program helped to preserve a delicate consensus in support of the government's overall China policy, a consensus that was shattered by the Tiananmen Incident of 1989. American friends of Taiwan could rest assured that its security would not be sacrificed in any hurried effort to further US-PRC ties.

Ironically, America's technological assistance and technology transfers to Taiwan may have helped to pave the way for increased US-PRC military cooperation. Fearing for Taiwan's security, in 1986, members of the US Congress threatened to torpedo the Reagan administration's proposed plans to provide the PRC with a US $550 million avionics modernization package for its high-altitude F-8 interceptor. After meeting with Department of State and Department of Defense officials, however, these individuals withdrew their objections. The representatives had apparently learned of classified projects designed to boost the defensive capabilities of Taiwan. Representative Mark D. Siljander (Republican–Michigan) explained:

The specifics of [the] agreements are classified upon the request of the Department of State, the administration, and the Defense Department, the specifics. We did, however—I want to make this clear in the general sense—receive important assurances that our relationship with Taiwan regarding defense as outlined in the Taiwan Relations Act will be met, and will be met in full.[82]

Given the fact that the representatives had opposed the F-8 modernization packages because it might cause Taiwan's air force to lose its qualitative air-superiority edge over the PRC, it is likely that Siljander was referring to classified agreements pertaining to America's assistance and support for Taiwan's IDF program.

An Attractive Alternative to Arms Sales

The US government recognizes the legal primacy of the TRA over the 1982 US-PRC Joint Communiqué. During congressional hearings, administration officials admitted that the communiqué should be considered as little more than a "modus vivendi," an "understanding" or a "statement of future policy."[83] Until such time as the US Congress decides to amend, revise or revoke the TRA, the American government is bound by statute to ensure that

Taiwan maintains a sufficient self-defense capability. Technological assistance and technology transfers to Taiwan have provided Washington with an attractive alternative to arms sales. The PRC's responses to the most "serious problem" in US-PRC relations have been decidedly low-key. Beijing's protestations lack the threatening tone of earlier diatribes against American arms sales to Taiwan. Indeed, a scathing attack upon present American policy was officially withdrawn two days after it appeared in the November 5, 1988, edition of the PRC journal, *Outlook (Liaowang).*[84]

A variety of factors may help to explain the PRC's surprisingly mild response to this issue. Regardless of Chinese public statements to the contrary, Beijing officials may have concluded privately that the transfer of American technology to Taiwan is not specifically prohibited by the 1982 communiqué. More likely, however, is the possibility that PRC officials may have sensed that Washington is determined not to budge on this issue.[85] Turning the subject into a major issue of contention might lead ultimately to a further deterioration in US-PRC relations. The PRC could lose its access to lucrative American markets. Finally, the technology-transfer arrangement allowed all parties involved in the matter to avoid losing face over the issue. The US took solace in the fact that it was abiding by the provisions of the TRA. The PRC congratulated itself upon having successfully convinced the US to reduce its arms sales to Taiwan. Taiwan could rest assured that it had not been abandoned by the US and that it will be able to maintain a sufficient, albeit expensive, defensive capability.

CONCLUSION

The principal reason the United States has assisted Taiwan in its drive for defense self-sufficiency is that the policy serves so many American interests. The policy has helped to promote regional peace and prosperity by ensuring that the costs of any PRC invasion or blockade of Taiwan remain prohibitively high. The policy has also provided the US with crucial leverage and a bargaining chip in its relations with both the PRC and Taiwan. This leverage may be employed to reduce some of the risks outlined above. Furthermore, during the mid-1980s, the policy helped to preserve a delicate domestic consensus in support of overall U.S. China policy. Finally, the policy provided the US with a viable and ingenious alternative to the more visible and controversial arms transfers.

Based upon the above analysis, it would appear likely that the American policy of assisting Taiwan in its drive for defense self-sufficiency will remain in place for the foreseeable future. However, it is not a perfect policy. The policy also holds numerous risks for the United States, including the possibility that some key programs in Taiwan's drive for defense self-sufficiency—particularly the development of a sophisticated fighter plane—may be infeasible and doomed to failure.

By the early 1990s, numerous technical difficulties, including the crash of an IDF prototype during a test flight in 1991, caused Taiwan officials to take a second look at the IDF project. Military authorities, believing that the aircraft's most serious problems are associated with the engine's propulsion power, have developed plans to upgrade the fighter and replace its Garrett-designed TFE1042 engine with a General Electric J101SF engine. Despite these moves, however, critics of the IDF program remain skeptical.

Some voices on Taiwan have charged that the IDF aircraft's initials really stand for "It Don't Fly."[86] US Defense Department officials have also criticized the plane, with one even describing it as "an underpowered Mattel version of the F-16."[87] The following chapter will explore the Bush administration's 1992 decision to provide Taiwan with an alternative to the IDF—advanced F-16 fighter aircraft.

Notes

1. "Weinberger Says US to Continue Support for ROC's Defense System," *China Post* (International Airmail Edition), May 30, 1988, p. 1.

2. For a complete text of the act, see Appendix 1.

3. For a complete text of the communiqué, see Appendix 2.

4. Christian Catrina, *Arms Transfers and Dependence* (New York: Taylor and Francis, 1988), p. 84.

5. Janne E. Nolan, *Military Industry in Taiwan and South Korea* (New York: St. Martin's Press, 1986), p. 28.

6. Nayan Chanda, "A Technical Point: US Rejects China's Stance on Technology Transfers to Taiwan," *Far Eastern Economic Review*, August 28, 1986, p. 26.

7. Private correspondence between Jim LeMunyon, Acting Assistant Secretary, United State Department of Commerce, and Senator John C. Danforth (Republican–Missouri), October 29, 1992, discussing the author's request for a list of approved export licenses granted for Taiwan during the period of 1988 through 1991. Letter provided courtesy of Senator Danforth's office.

8. See Robert Karniol, "Using the Loophole," *Far Eastern Economic Review*, July 30, 1987, p. 17 and "US Arms Sales to Taiwan Top 4190m," *Jane's Defence Weekly*, December 24, 1988, p. 1584.

9. "Weinberger Says US to Continue Support."

10. "Defense Committee Holds 1st Meeting Open to Reporters," *China Post* (International Airmail Edition), November 17, 1988, p. 1.

11. See "Taiwan's Ching-Kuo fighter," *Jane's Defence Weekly*, January 7, 1989, p. 4. However, according to official sources in Taipei, development of the aircraft began in 1983. See "ROC-Designed Fighter to Be Flying by Year End," *China Post* (International Airmail Edition), October 10, 1988, p. 1.

12. "Peking Might Be Eyeing an Invasion of Taiwan, with World's Attention Focused on Middle East," *Free China Journal*, November 19, 1990, p. 2.

13. By the late 1980s, the US had shut down all of its F-5E and F-104 production lines.

14. "First ROC-Developed Jet Unveiled in Taichung," *China Post* (International Airmail Edition), December 12, 1988, p. 4.

15. See "Defense Ministry Gunning to Improve Public Image," *Free China Journal*, August 23, 1990, p. 2.

16. "Taiwan's Ching-kuo Fighter," *Jane's Defence Weekly*, January 7, 1989, p. 4.

17. Ibid.

18. Arthur Cheng, "The IDF Close Up," *Sinorama* 16, no. 4 (April 1991): p. 29.

19. See Mark Lambert (ed.), *Jane's: All the World's Aircraft, 1991-92* (Alexandria, Virginia: Jane's Information Group, 1991), p. 227.

20. See "IDF Production Faces 50% Cut," *China Post* (International Airmail Edition), March 24, 1993, p. 4.

21. "First ROC-Developed Jet Unveiled in Taichung," *China Post* (International Airmail Edition), December 12, 1988, p. 4.

22. Ibid.

23. Ibid.

24. Ta Yu-shan, "IDF Upgrade Program to Continue," *China Post* (International Airmail Edition), September 5, 1992, p. 4.

25. After saying that "a lot of technology has already been transferred to Taiwan" and that "jobs are very important in the US at this point," representatives of General Dynamics ruled out the possibility that major technology transfers will accompany the sale of the F-16s to Taiwan. For more information, see Rodney Chan, "No Technology Transfer from US," *China Post* (International Airmail Edition), September 5, 1992, p. 1.

26. *Jane's Weapons Systems: 1988-1989* (Alexandria, Virginia: Jane's Publishing Company, Ltd., 1989), p. 126.

27. "Taiwan-Based Missiles Can Defend Island: Chen," *Free China Journal*, November 11, 1990, p. 2.

28. Robert Karniol, "Taiwan's Warheads," *Far Eastern Economic Review*, July 30, 1987, p. 18.

29. Ibid.

30. See ROC Ministry of Defense, *1992 National Defense Report, Republic of China* (Taipei: Li Ming Cultural Enterprise Corporation, 1992), p. 151. Translated from the Chinese by Ma Kainan, Major General, ROC Army. Known as the "Defense White Paper," this publication is also available in Chinese.

31. For more information, see "US Patriot Missile's Brains OK for Taiwan: Pentagon Approves Guidance System sale for ROC Sky Bow," *Free China Journal*, January 17, 1992, p. 2 and Jim Mann, "US to Sell Missile Parts to Taiwan," *China Post* (International Airmail Edition), January 13, 1992, p. 1. Also see, "Report: US Will Sell Patriot missiles to ROC," *China Post* (International Airmail Edition), January 8, 1993, p. 1.

32. Quoted from David Hughes, "Taiwan to Acquire Patriot Derivative," *Aviation Week and Space Technology*, March 1, 1993, p. 61.

33. *Jane's Weapon Systems: 1988–89*, p. 698.

34. ROC Ministry of Defense, *1992 National Defense Report*, p. 155.

35. Cheng, "The IDF Close Up," p. 29.

36. "Cabinet Reports: Anti-Ship Missile Developed by ROC," *China Post* (International Airmail Edition) September 7, 1988, p. 1.

37. *Jane's Weapons Systems: 1988–89*, p. 455.

38. See "New Weapons Developed to Protect Taiwan, Defense Ministry Reports," *Free China Journal*, March 25, 1991, p. 2.

39. See Hsieh Shu-fen, "Overcoming Adversity on the Seas—The Navy Plans for the Future," *Sinorama* 16, no. 9 (September 1991): 85.

40. See Institute for Strategic Studies, *The Military Balance: 1991–1992*, (London: Brassey's, 1991), p. 180.

41. Hsieh, "Overcoming Adversity on the Seas," p. 85.

42. Martin L. Lasater, *Policy in Evolution: The U.S. Role in China's Reunification* (Boulder, Colorado: Westview Press, 1989), p. 174.

43. Hsieh, "Overcoming Adversity on the Seas," pp. 89–90.

44. For more information, see "'Cheng Kung-1101' makes naval debut," *China Post* (International Airmail Edition), May 8, 1993, p. 1.

45. See International Institute for Strategic Studies, *The Military Balance, 1991-1992*, p. 180.

46. Robert Karniol, "New Arms for Old," *Far Eastern Economic Review*, July 30, 1987, p. 15.

47. For more information, see "'Brave Tiger' Tank Roars," *Free China Journal*, April 19, 1990, p. 1.

48. See International Institute for Strategic Studies, *The Military Balance: 1991–1992*, p. 180, and "ROC 'Elite' Force Protects Taiwan," *Free China Journal*, February 28, 1992, p. 7.

49. See Tai Ming Cheung, "Still Gung-ho," *Far Eastern Economic Review*, May 18, 1989, p. 23.

50. Ibid.

51. Peter Kien-hong Yu, "Arms Balance Peace Insurance," *Free China Journal*, November 26, 1990, p. 5.

52. "ROC Capable of Producing Nuclear Arms," *China Post* (International Airmail Edition), December 12, 1988, p. 1.

53. Lincoln Kaye, "Atomic Intentions," *Far Eastern Economic Review*, May 3, 1990, p. 9.

54. "ROC Ready for Communist Attack, NDS Told," *China Post* (International Airmail Edition), July 27, 1988, p. 1.

55. Ibid.

56. For more information, see "Taiwan-Based Missiles Can Defend Island: Chen," *Free China Journal*, November 1, 1990, p. 2.

57. Yu, "Arms Balance Peace Insurance," p. 5.

58. In an agreement similar to that with the US for the Perry-class frigates, the French will not provide armaments for the ships. For more information, see "France Approves Sale of 16 Frigate Hulls for ROC Navy," *Free China Journal*, October 1, 1991, p. 2 and H. K. Cheng, "Military Confirms French Ship Deal," *China Post* (International Airmail Edition), March 9, 1992, p. 4.

59. Selig Harrison, "Interview/Hu Yaobang: Peking Lashes Out at Washington-Taipei links," *Far Eastern Economic Review*, July 24, 1986, pp. 26-27.

60. Quoted from Martin L. Lasater, "United States Arms Sales to Taiwan," in Steven W. Mosher (ed.), *The United States and the Republic of China: Democratic Friends, Strategic Allies and Economic Partners*, (New Brunswick, New Jersey: Transaction Publishers, 1992), p. 120.

61. See Harrison, "Interview/Hu Yaobang," pp. 26-27.

62. "Beijing Concerns Sale of Missile Parts to Taiwan," *China Post* (International Airmail Edition), January 17, 1992, p. 1.

63. *Defense and Foreign Affairs Handbook, 1987-88 Edition* (Washington, D.C.: Perth Corporation, 1987), p. 203.

64. Cheng, "The IDF Close Up," p. 29.

65. Paul Proctor, "IDF Fighter Program Provides Catalyst for Advanced Manufacturing Capability," *Aviation Week and Space Technology*, April 27, 1992, p. 39.

66. Joel Millman, "Taiwan's Central American Links," *Jane's Defense Weekly*, November 26, 1988, p. 1330.

67. An unidentified Bush administration official charged that Iraq had acquired military equipment and poison gas materials from Libya, Yemen, South Africa and Taiwan. For more information, see Lisa Beyer, "The Center Holds for Now," *Time*, September 3, 1990, p. 35.

68. "Time's ROC-Iraq Report 'Groundless:' Officials," *Free China Journal*, September 6, 1990, p. 1.

69. "New Weapons Development to Protect Taiwan," Defense Ministry Reports," *Free China Journal*, March 25, 1991, p. 2.

70. For more information, see Annie Huang, "Taiwan Bank Asked to Settle Arms Deal Lawsuit with Iran," *China Post* (International Airmail Edition), March 28, 1992, p. 1.

71. Nolan, *Military Industry*, pp. 12–13.

72. A. James Gregor and Maria Hsia Chang, "Taiwan: The 'Wild Card' in U.S. Defense Policy in the Far Pacific," in James C. Hsiung and Winberg Chai (eds.), *Asia and U.S. Foreign Policy* (New York: Praeger, 1981), p. 138.

73. Ibid., p. 140.

74. See "Lawmakers Slash Military Budget," *China Post* (International Airmail Edition), April 27, 1992, p. 4.

75. See material submitted for the record by Martin L. Lasater in *Implementation of the Taiwan Relations Act*, Hearing and Markup before the Committee on Foreign Relations and Its Subcommittee on Human Rights and International Organizations and on Asian and Pacific Affairs of the House of Representatives, 99th Congress, 2d on H. Con. Res. 223 and H. Con. Res. 334, May 7, June 25, August 1, 1986, p. 145.

76. "ROC Armed Forces Could Fend Off M'land Invasion," *China Post* (International Airmail Edition), April 11, 1989, p. 1.

77. See Prepared Statement of Representative Mark D. Siljander (Republican–Michigan) in *Implementation of the Taiwan Relations Act*, p. 46.

78. "Mainland Official Says: Invasion of Taiwan Not Worth the Money," *China Post* (International Airmail Edition), September 27, 1988, p. 1.

79. See "Defense Boss: Problems Dog Airspace Defense," *China Post* (International Airmail Edition), March 29, 1993, p. 4.

80. See Department of Defense, "A Strategic Framework for the Asian Pacific Rim: Looking Toward the 21st Century," in *The President's Report on the Military Presence in East Asia*, Hearings Before the Committee on Armed Services, United States Senate, 101st Congress, 2d Session, April 19, 1990, pp. 31–55.

81. Interestingly, John Copper has suggested that the US has used its arms exports to promote democracy on Taiwan. For more information, see John F. Copper, *China Diplomacy: The Washington-Taipei-Beijing Triangle*, (Boulder, Colorado: Westview Press, 1992), pp. 120–124.

82. Testimony of Representative Mark D. Siljander (Republican–Michigan) in *Implementation of the Taiwan Relations Act*, p. 43.

83. See testimony of John H. Holdridge, Assistant Secretary of the Bureau of East Asian and Pacific Affairs, Department of State, in *China and Taiwan*, Hearing Before the Committee on Foreign Relations, United States Senate, 97th Congress, 2d Session, August 17, 1982 p. 13.

84. See Nayan Chanda, "A Technical Point: US Rejects China's Stance on Technology Transfers to Taiwan," *Far Eastern Economic Review*, August 28, 1986, p. 26.

85. For more information, see Martin L. Lasater, "US Arms Sales to Taiwan," in Steven W. Mosher *The United States and the Republic of China*, pp. 120–121.

86. See "This Sale Is a Mirage," *Time*, July 13, 1992, p. 9.

87. Jim Mann, "Taiwan to U.S.: We're Back!" *Los Angeles Times*, July 28, 1992, p. 4.

5

The Sale of F-16 Fighters to Taiwan

On September 2, 1992, President George Bush announced that he would approve the sale of up to 150 F-16 fighter jets to Taiwan, a move that some contend reverses ten years of American arms sales policy. This chapter examines the Bush administration's decision to provide Taiwan with sophisticated warplanes. It explores the terms of the agreement, analyzes a variety of considerations that may have led the US to equip Taiwan with advanced fighters and discusses whether this move violates the 1982 US-PRC Joint Communiqué, a document in which the US promised to "reduce gradually its sales of arms to Taiwan."

THE F-16 AIRCRAFT AGREEMENT

For over a decade, Taiwan sought unsuccessfully to purchase jet fighters from the US. Indeed, as recently as June 1992, Washington had turned down Taipei's request for F-16s.[1] Therefore, President Bush's announcement that he would lift the

ban on the sale of warplanes came as an unexpected relief to
Taiwan's leaders. In addition to 150 F-16/A and F-16/B aircraft,
the US $6 billion deal includes 40 spare engines, 900 Sidewinder
missiles, 600 Sparrow missiles, 500,000 rounds of 20-mm cannon
shells, spare parts, technical documentation and logistics service
and personnel training.[2]

First developed by General Dynamics in 1972, the F-16/A and
F-16/B fighters are one-seater and two-seater aircraft respectively.
The jets have a thrust power of approximately 10,000 kilograms
and a radius of action of about 925 kilometers. Although these
warplanes are formidable dogfighters, many analysts consider
them inferior to the later model F-16/C and F-16/D types that are
equipped with improved fire radar controls and
beyond-visual-range air-to-air missiles. Consequently, some ROC
officials, including Lin Wen-li, Commanding General of Taiwan's
air force, complained that "We are not very satisfied with the A
and B models."[3]

Sensitive to Taipei's complaints, but unwilling to provide it
with the F-16/C or F-16/D, the US has agreed to sell updated
versions of the F-16/A and F-16/B. The warplanes will be
equipped with the F-16 mid-life upgrade (MLU)—an upgrade
program developed originally for NATO forces in Europe. MLU
modifications include "a cockpit similar to the F-16/D Block 50's
with wide angle head-up display, night vision goggle
compatibility, modular mission computer, digital terrain
navigation system, AN/APG 66 (V2A) radar upgrade, GPS
navigation system, improved data modem and provision for a
microwave landing system."[4]

It is also noteworthy that the jets will be powered by an
upgraded version of the original F-16 engine—a Pratt and
Whitney F100-PW-220 afterburning turbofan unit. According to
John Balaguer, President of Pratt and Whitney's Government and
Space Propulsion Division, the 220 model "embodies
state-of-the-art technology, derived from our newest generation
of fighter power plants."[5] Although the engine is less powerful
than the General Electric unit that powers the F-16/C and

F-16/D, representatives of General Dynamics claim that its lighter weight makes the plane more agile and provides it with an advantage in maneuverability, making it a better warplane for air-to-air missions.[6] The proposed sale passed the required 30-day congressional notification period without opposition. The deal was officially completed when formal letters of offer and acceptance for the planes, engines and other equipment were signed by US and Taiwan representatives on November 12 and 13, 1992. Deliveries are expected to begin in 1996 and continue for a period of several years.

MOTIVATIONS FOR THE F-16 SALE

Why has the US agreed to provide Taiwan with advanced fighter aircraft? What does America hope to gain by such a policy? As with any other new initiative, many questions have been raised. The following discussion analyzes several considerations that may have influenced US policy.

PRC Arms Buildup

Since the early 1980s, the PRC has sought to modernize its armed forces. The People's Liberation Army's (PLA) embarrassing performance during its 1979 attempt to "teach Vietnam a lesson" served to underscore a pressing need for military modernization. After the Sino-Vietnamese war, American military specialists traveled to China and identified the following as among major sources of weakness in the PLA:

Lack of mobility and mechanization; poor logistics systems for sustained offensive operations; marginal C3 [command, control and communications] capability; obsolete weaponry; limited power projection capability; obsolescent aircraft and avionics; poor pilot training; inadequate communications; limited defense industry capability; obsolescent ship and onboard equipment; limited amphibious lift capability.[7]

The stunning show of American technology during the Persian Gulf War further demonstrated to Beijing's leadership the obsolescence of the PLA's equipment. One Chinese source observed, "after the Gulf War, Chinese leaders pushed very hard to modernize [the PLA]. . . . They saw the importance of high-tech weapons."[8]

The collapse of the Soviet Union has proved to be a bonanza for China's military. According to one Bush administration source, PRC officials "are going into the former Soviet Union and picking the shelves clean at fire sale prices—they are buying not only weapons, but advanced technologies so that they can upgrade their own weapons."[9] The total outflow of arms and military technology is difficult to gauge. However, US officials confirm that recent Chinese arms purchases include a squadron of 24 Sukhoi 27 Flanker jet fighters (an advanced all-weather air-to-air warplane with a range of more than 2,400 miles), S-300 surface-to-air missiles, heavy transport aircraft and Mi-17 Hip helicopters. Technological acquisitions include air-to-air refueling capabilities, missile guidance technology, rocket technology and submarine and anti-submarine warfare technology. Moreover, authorities suspect that Beijing is negotiating with Russian officials for the purchase of MiG-29 "Fulcrum" and MiG-31 "Foxhound" aircraft, T-72 main battle tanks, a partially completed aircraft carrier and the production technology required to assemble MiG-31 fighters.[10]

China's neighbors view the military buildup with alarm. After learning of the PRC's acquisition of advanced Soviet aircraft, Albert Lin, Taiwan's spokesman in Washington, D.C., exclaimed that "somehow, somewhere, we have to get new aircraft."[11] Japanese officials have informed Washington, Moscow and Beijing that Tokyo is also worried about the arms purchases.[12] Indeed, most powers actively engaged in the Pacific region—including Vietnam, Japan, Taiwan, South Korea and the United States—share this concern. Taeho Kim, a South Korean defense analyst, observed, "Virtually every nation in East Asia can agree that the People's Republic of China's growing naval and air-strike capabilities will become a significant concern in the minds of strategic planners."[13]

Does the PRC's arms buildup best explain Washington's decision to provide Taiwan with advanced fighter aircraft? When announcing the sale, President Bush only hinted at the role that the Chinese military buildup had played in his decision. He stated that the sale would "help maintain peace and stability in an area of great concern to us."[14] Other officials were more direct. In August 1992, during an appearance on the US television program "Meet the Press," Brent Scowcroft, President Bush's National Security Advisor, revealed that the administration "had decided to review its policy of not selling F-16s to Taiwan mainly because China had purchased advanced fighters from Russia."[15] After Bush's announcement, Pentagon spokesman, Robert Hall, defended the move by noting that "a discrepancy is building" between the air force capabilities of Taiwan and PRC.[16] Joe Snyder, spokesperson for the Department of State, also conceded that "the aging of Taiwan's air force and China's purchase of Russian Su-27 aircraft were among the factors considered in the President's decision."[17]

Domestic Politics

With the end of the cold war, manufacturers of advanced warplanes—including Dassault in France and General Dynamics in the US—have found that demand for new fighter aircraft has declined. In mid-1992, General Dynamics announced that, with the possible end of new F-16 orders, it would have to layoff 5,800 employees at its Fort Worth, Texas, plant by the mid-1990s. Scores of workers at F-16 suppliers scattered throughout 47 other states would also lose their jobs.

As word of the F-16-related layoffs spread, Representatives Joe Barton (Republican–Texas) and Pete Geren (Democrat–Texas) spearheaded an intense congressional campaign to pressure the Bush administration to lift the ban on advanced fighter sales to Taiwan. In August 1992, 100 members of the House of Representatives (53 Democrats and 47 Republicans) signed a letter demanding that the President approve the F-16 sales and warning that "if we do not allow F-16 sales to Taiwan, they will buy French aircraft and will also make a commitment to purchase French nuclear power plants and railroad technology."[18] As Representative Barton noted, the letter was signed by "everybody from Barney Frank to Newt Gingrich. . . . This is one of those funny issues where the far left and far right, for different reasons, come to the same conclusion."[19] The Barton-Geren petition was followed by a second appeal stressing that "if the US does not make this sale, the business—and the jobs—will go to other countries. . . . Whether we sell [Taiwan] F-15s, F-16s or F-18s does not matter, what does matter is that [Taiwan] purchases American aircraft produced by American workers."[20]

Others joined in the effort to persuade President Bush to permit the arms sales. During congressional hearings, Senator Lloyd Bentsen (Democrat–Texas) described the F-16 deal as "a dream sale" and criticized the administration's refusal to approve it as "a senseless . . . dumb policy."[21] Governor Ann Richards (Democrat–Texas) accused the President of failing to deal in the global marketplace and complained that "I don't know what deals have been made between George Bush and Communist China, but when it means the loss of 5,800 workers in Fort Worth, Texas, it's time to wake up and smell the coffee."[22] Dean Girardot, a spokesman for the International Association of Machinists, the labor union that represents about 10,000 General Dynamics employees, was even more direct. The labor leader bluntly called on the President to "get off his duff and let General Dynamics sell these F-16s to Taiwan."[23]

The President's decision to approve the F-16 sales to Taiwan enjoyed widespread bipartisan political support. Even Governor

Bill Clinton of Arkansas, then the Democratic candidate for President, supported the move. But many also questioned the President's motives. The fact that Bush chose to permit the sales during the midst of his faltering re-election campaign—and made his announcement on the same day that he approved massive wheat subsidies for South Dakota farmers and a huge F-15 fighter sale to Saudi Arabia—made it appear as though he was attempting primarily to capture Texas' 32 electoral votes. An editorial in the *New York Times* opined that Bush's election-year arms sales seemed "to have been driven exclusively by an effort to secure jobs and votes at home."[24] Senator Bentsen observed that, while he was happy that the President finally approved the F-16 sales, "it sure took a lot of pressure in an election year by me and the Texas delegation to persuade him."[25]

Foreign observers also suspected that presidential politics played a critical role in Bush's decision. One Japanese official suggested that American foreign policy was "being held hostage to domestic elections."[26] Authorities in the PRC charged that Bush was attempting to "meet the wishes of some corporations that stand to gain" and warned that he would not improve his re-election chances with the sale.[27]

The End of the Cold War

After negotiating the 1982 US-PRC Joint Communiqué—an agreement that seemed to commit the US to reduce its arms sales to Taiwan—Reagan administration officials defended the controversial initiative by arguing that "our foreign policy objective was to preserve a valuable and strategic relationship [with the PRC] which otherwise might well, and probably would, have undergone a serious and possibly fatal deterioration."[28] At the time, maintenance of Beijing's support for Washington's global drive to contain the spread of Soviet influence represented a critical element in American strategic thinking.

The collapse of the Soviet Union, an event that brought an end to the era of intense superpower rivalry, reduced China's strategic importance to the US. American officials who might have opposed the sale of advanced aircraft to Taiwan during the Cold War now supported the move. Indeed, according to one account, "This time almost no one in the bureaucracy argued against antagonizing the Chinese by ending the United States' 10-year ban on weapons sales to Taipei."[29]

Other Considerations

Numerous other considerations might also have influenced US policy. Taiwan's media boasted that "a major reason" for the Bush administration's approval of the F-16 sales was "Taipei's persistent lobbying . . . which demonstrates that only through our own persistent work can we earn international support."[30] Others suggested that the sale was motivated by an effort to retain a significant degree of influence over the nature and direction of Taiwan's military buildup. According to this view, "as long as we are the only supplier to Taiwan, then there's some control over things. . . . If there are no controls, then anybody will sell anything to Taiwan—the French, the Russians, anyone."[31] Finally, some defense experts believed that the sale would help to reduce objections to the renewal of military ties with Beijing.[32] Interestingly, on December 22, 1992, the Bush administration did resume arms shipments to the PRC. Equipment slated for delivery included "four anti-submarine torpedoes, two artillery-loading radars, equipment for a munitions-production line and electronic gear to upgrade F-8 aircraft."[33]

Summary

In sum, no single factor led the Bush administration to lift the ban on the sale of advanced fighter aircraft to Taiwan. Even those who charge that the move was "sheer political expediency" concede that "you can go beyond the political factors and find some fairly good policy reasons for it."[34] But while many factors played a role in the decision, strategic and domestic political considerations were the driving force. Other factors—including Taiwan's persistent lobbying and a desire by the US to retain some control over the direction of Taiwan's drive for military modernization—may have also helped to influence policy.

THE F-16 SALE AND THE 1982 US-PRC JOINT COMMUNIQUE'

In 1982, the US and the PRC negotiated a joint communiqué that focused on the overall issue of continued American arms transfers to Taiwan. Does the sale of 150 upgraded F-16/A and F-16/B aircraft—warplanes far superior to anything in Taiwan's existing inventory—violate the terms of this agreement?

A Violation of the Communiqué

Authorities in the PRC contend that the Bush administration's decision to sell advanced warplanes to Taiwan is a direct violation of the 1982 communiqué. PRC Vice Foreign Minister Liu Hua-qui charges that the sale "completely violates" the document.[35] Moreover, Beijing's official Xinhua news agency has branded the Bush administration's efforts to justify the sale as fabricated "excuses and lies."[36]

Some Americans agree with this assessment. Professor A. Doak Barnett of Johns Hopkins University, described by the *Washington Post* as "the dean of US China watchers," said that the sale amounts to "the abrogation" of the communiqué.[37] Tanya L. Domi, an arms transfer analyst at the Council for a Livable World Education Fund in Washington, D.C., believes that "the F-16 sale clearly violates this agreement."[38]   Morton I. Abramowitz, president of the Carnegie Endowment for International Peace, opined that the President's action "massively violate[s] a written agreement."[39]

Not a Violation of the Communiqué

When President Bush approved the sale of F-16 fighter aircraft in Fort Worth, Texas, he stated that the initiative did not violate any existing agreements with the PRC:

> My decision today does not change the commitment of this administration and its predecessors to the three Communiqués with the PRC.   We keep our word: our one-China policy, our recognition of the PRC as the sole legitimate government of China. I've always stressed that the importance of the 1982 Communiqué on arms sales to Taiwan lies in its promotion of common political goals: peace and stability in the area through mutual respect.[40]

Since that time, US officials have not budged from this position.

US authorities have employed a number of arguments in an effort to defend the view that the sale of advanced warplanes to Taiwan "is fully in keeping with the spirit and the letter of the communiqué."[41]   Officials contend that the original 1982 agreement provides for the one-for-one replacement of Taiwan's military equipment and that Washington may provide Taiwan with upgraded weapons when spare parts for existing systems become unavailable.   Because American firms no longer manufacture parts for Taiwan's obsolete F-5E and F-104 fighters, new F-16s were the only practical alternative.   Joe Snyder, spokesman for the Department of State, explains:

> We said we would be providing spare parts, and so forth.   It's impossible now to provide spare parts for the old aircraft that they have, and we're maintaining the quality of that air force in the only way that we have available now.[42]

In this respect, the F-16 sale is not without precedent. During the 1980s, the US quietly sold upgraded transport planes to Taiwan when spare parts for older aircraft became unavailable.[43] American officials also claim that the central goal of the communiqué is to promote "peace and stability." The F-16 aircraft sale advances this objective by restoring the military balance across the Taiwan Strait. As Lawrence Eagleburger, then acting Secretary of State, explained, "In fact, when these aircraft are on the ground in Taiwan, it will only put the Taiwanese air force back at about the strength it was in 1980."[44]

Analysis

Taken at face value, the PRC's position that the F-16 sale "completely violates" the terms of the 1982 US-PRC Communiqué has substantial merit. Even a cursory glance at the document reveals that it does not address the issue of replacement parts for Taiwan's aircraft, new planes or the balance of military forces across the Taiwan Strait. Furthermore, despite the comments of US officials, it is clear that the central issue addressed in the accord is the topic of continued American arms transfers to Taiwan—not peace and stability.

A close examination of US documents pertaining to the meaning of the communiqué, however, shows that the American view also has validity. During 1982 and 1983, congressional hearings were held to investigate the terms of the document. As one official noted at the time, these hearings served the important purpose of establishing a record that accompanies the communiqué.[45] Significantly, the issue of the maintenance of the military balance across the Taiwan Strait was addressed during these proceedings.

From the outset, Washington has maintained the position that the 1982 communiqué permits it to upgrade Taiwan's defensive capabilities (both quantitatively and qualitatively) if the PRC strengthens its military power. During congressional hearings,

John Holdridge, Assistant Secretary for the Bureau of East Asian
and Pacific Affairs, Department of State, was asked whether the
US reserved the right to elevate arms sales to Taiwan if the PRC
increased its military capabilities. Holdridge testified:

Let us say that everything is predicated again on the military
situation and the political situation attendant to the Taiwan Strait and
the Taiwan question. Again, we will make our judgments based
upon these conditions and act accordingly.[46]

In a written response to a question that focused on the quality
of US arms sales to Taiwan, the Department of State voiced a
similar interpretation. When asked whether the US could sell
Taiwan "what is necessary to maintain the current balance" across
the Taiwan Strait, department officials replied:

We will continue to monitor not only China's announced intentions
but also its military capability and the manner in which that
capability is deployed. Should it become apparent that China's
policy has changed or is changing, we would naturally feel free to
reassess our policy.[47]

President Reagan also seemed to leave the door open for
advanced weapons sales to Taiwan when he was asked during an
interview whether Washington would "still go along with the
idea" that Taiwan's defenses could not be upgraded, if the PRC
decided to "increase and modernize it's military arsenal." The
President replied, "No, we're doing all the things that we have
always done."[48] When asked later during the same interview
whether the US is "allowed to upgrade Taiwan's defenses,
especially if the Mainland upgrades its defenses," Reagan
answered, "We're giving them what we mutually agree upon
when their people come here and sit down and go over their
defense needs, and as the Taiwan Relations Act requires, we will
continue to address their capabilities and their needs dependent on
the situation in the region."[49]

CONCLUSION

Since the signing of the 1982 communiqué, the US and the PRC have quarreled about the meaning of it. A 1983 study by the Senate Judiciary Committee's Subcommittee on the Separation of Powers found that Beijing and Washington "publicly disagree on the meaning of every significant pronouncement in the document."[50] Because the two sides have never agreed on the significance or purpose of the communiqué, it remains an open question as to what exactly constitutes a violation of the accord. However, a review of US documents pertaining to the meaning of the communiqué shows that the F-16 sale is consistent with America's long-standing interpretation of the accord and its commitment to the security of Taiwan.

When President Bush announced that he would lift the decade-old ban on advanced fighter aircraft sales to Taiwan, some predicted that the PRC would "scream like a scalded cat."[51] Perhaps cognizant of its weak bargaining position in relation to the US, however, China took only minor steps in retaliation for the sale. These included a temporary boycott of the "Big Five" (US, Russia, China, France and Great Britain) talks on nuclear proliferation in the Middle East and the rejection of a proposal for a Chinese-American human rights commission. Rather than downgrade relations, the PRC "made a huge purchase of American wheat and bought six Boeing passenger airliners in what seemed to be a peace offering to President-elect Bill Clinton."[52]

The F-16 sale seems to have helped pave the way for other arms sales. Shortly after the F-16 announcement, the US agreed to sell Patriot missiles and sophisticated anti-submarine helicopters to Taipei. Furthermore, in November 1992, *Defense News* reported that the Dutch and German governments might lift their ban on arms sales to Taiwan and permit their ship-building industries to submit bids for Taiwan's next major arms project—the purchase of ten non-nuclear submarines worth approximately US $5 billion.[53] The most significant development, however, came in January 1993 when France formally announced that it had approved the sale of 60 Mirage 2000-5 fighters to Taiwan. When defending the sale, French officials indicated "that Paris would not stand for mainland China retaliating against France if it failed to punish the United States for selling 150 F-16 fighters to Taipei."[54] Ironically, Tian Qin-ming, the PRC's embassy spokesman in Paris, retorted that the French and American sales "took place in different historical contexts" and that the US aircraft deal "should be within limits set by the August 1982 Sino-American Communiqué."[55]

Notes

1. See Barbara Starr and John Boatman, "US Reconsiders F-16 Sale Ban," *Jane's Defence Weekly*, August 8, 1992, p. 5.
2. See Michael Towle, "Taiwan Hopes Election Pressure Will Aid F-16 Sale," *Fort Worth Star-Telegram*, September 19, 1992, p. B1.
3. P. T. Bangsberg, "Sale of F-16 Jets to Taiwan Strains US-China Relations," *Journal of Commerce*, September 4, 1992, p. 3A.
4. Joris Janssen Lok, "US Benefits from European MLU," *Jane's Defence Weekly*, November 14, 1992, p. 8.
5. Tammy C. Peng, "F-16 Contract Finalized: Delivery to Begin in 1996," *Free China Journal*, November 17, 1992, p. 2.
6. Michael Towle, "Taiwan Hopes Election Pressure," p. B1.
7. See Prepared Statement of Mark D. Siljander (Republican-Michigan) in *Implementation of the Taiwan Relations Act*, Hearing and Markup Before the Committee on Foreign Affairs and Its Subcommittee on Human Rights and International Organizations and on Asian and Pacific Affairs of the House of Representatives, 99th Congress, 2d Session on H. Con. Res. 233 and H. Con. Res. 334, May 7, June 25, August 1, 1986, p. 48.
8. Jim Mann, "China Seeks Russian Weapons in Effort to Modernize Military," *Los Angeles Times*, July 13, 1992, p. A3.
9. Thomas L. Friedman, "China Warns US on Taiwan Jet Deal," *New York Times*, September 4, 1992, p. A3.

10. For more information on China's military and technology purchases from the former Soviet Union, see Michael R. Gordon, "Moscow Is Selling Weapons to China, US Officials Say," *New York Times*, October 18, 1992, p. 1; Barbara Starr, "MiG Buy May Lead to Chinese Copies," *Jane's Defence Weekly*, October 10, 1992, p. 18 and Jim Mann and David Holley, "China Builds Military: Neighbors, U.S. Uneasy," *Los Angles Times*, September 13, 1992, p. A7.

11. Susumu Awanohara, "Election Dynamics: Candidate Bush to Review Aircraft Sale to Taiwan," *Far Eastern Economic Review*, August 20, 1992, p. 20.

12. See B.J. Cutler, "China's Ambitions Raise Tensions," *Washington Times*, July 19, 1992, p. B4 and "China Told Aircraft Carrier Purchase Would Be Destablizing," *Japan Times* (Weekly Edition), September 21-27, 1992, p. 3.

13. See Jim Mann and David Holley, "China Builds Military," p. A26.

14. "Remarks to General Dynamics Employees in Fort Worth, Texas, September 2, 1992," *Weekly Compilation of Presidential Documents: Monday* September 7, 1992, p. 1556. See Appendix to this book.

15. Daniel Southerland, "Ban on F-16 Sales to Taiwan May End," *Washington Post*, September 2, 1992, p. A25.

16. Barbara Starr, "F-16 Sale Justified by 'Discrepancy,'" *Jane's Defence Weekly*, September 12, 1992, p. 5.

17. Transcript of press briefing by Joe Snyder, Department of State, September 3, 1992. The transcript, provided courtesy of Department of State, is reprinted in this book as Appendix 4.

18. Jackie Koszczuk, "Lawmakers Urging Bush to Approve Sale of F-16s to Taiwan," *Fort Worth Star-Telegram*, August 19, 1992, p. 10.

19. Ibid.

20. "Bush Warned Against Losing Multibillion Dlr Sale to France," *China Post* (International Airmail Edition), August 19, 1992, p. 1.

21. Ibid.

22. "Bush Would Reconsider Selling F-16s to Taiwan," *China Post* (International Airmail Edition), August 1, 1992, p. 1.

23. Ibid.

24. Thomas Friedman, "Selling Arms to Keep Jobs: The Signals It Sends Abroad," *New York Times*, September 20, 1992, p. E4.

25. "Bush Approves Sale of F-16s," *China Post* (International Airmail Edition), September 3, 1992, p. 1.

26. Leslie Helm, "Taiwan Sale May Start Asian Arms Race," *Japan Times*, September 7, 1992, p. 19.

27. "China Warns US Trade Is Jeopardizes by Sale of Military Aircraft to Taiwan," *Japan Times*, September 9, 1992, p. 6.

28. See testimony of John H. Holdridge, Assistant Secretary, Bureau of East Asian and Pacific Affairs, Department of State, in *China and Taiwan*, Hearing Before the Committee on Foreign Relations, United States Senate, 97th Congress, 2d Session, August 17, 1982, p. 24.

29. Thomas L. Friedman, "China Warns US on Taiwan Jet Deal," p. 3A.

30. "Finally We Will Get F-16 Jets," *China Post* (International Airmail Edition), September 5, 1992, p. 2.

31. "Bush Approves Sale of F-16s," p. 1.

32. These individuals contend that "it is in the interest of the US as well as China that exchange of high-level military personnel and sales of US military equipment resume." For more information, see Susumu Awanohara, "Election Dynamics," p. 20.

33. Keith Bradsher, "US Will Release Weapons to China," *New York Times*, December 23, 1992, p. 1. Also see "Bush Lifts Ban on Arms Sales to the Chinese," *Washington Post*, December 23, 1992, p. A22.

34. See statement of David Scheffer quoted in James McGregor, "Beijing's Reliance on US Limits Response to Jet Sale," *Asian Wall Street Journal* (Weekly Edition), September 14, 1992, p. 2.

35. See David Holley, "China May Skip Arms Talks over Taiwan Jet Deal," *Los Angeles Times*, September 4, 1992, p. A3.

36. "China Says US Lies to Back-up F-16 Sale," *International Herald Tribune*, September 5, 1992, p. 5.

37. Don Oberdorfer, "US Decries China's Sale of Reactor, But Clears the Way for Satellite Deal," *Washington Post*, September 12, 1992, p. A13.

38. Tanya L. Domi, "Sale of Fighter Jets Harms US Credibility," *Christian Science Monitor*, October 20, 1992, p. 18.

39. Quoted from Thomas L. Friedman, "Selling Arms to Keep Jobs: The Signals It Sends Abroad," *New York Times*, September 20, 1992, p. E4.

40. "Remarks to General Dynamics Employees," p. 1557.

41. Joe Snyder employed these terms when defending the F-16 sales. See Transcript of press briefing by Joe Snyder in Appendix 4.

42. Ibid.

43. See Richard C. Bush, "The Role of the United States in Taiwan-PRC Relations," in Dennis Fred Simon and Michael Y. M. Kau, *Taiwan: Beyond the Economic Miracle* (Armonk, New York: M. E. Sharpe, 1992), p. 352.

44. See Susumu Awanohara and Julian Baum, "Pork Barrel Roll," *Far Eastern Economic Review*, September 17, 1992, p. 12.

45. See testimony of Paul D. Wolfowitz, Assistant Secretary of State for East Asian and Pacific Affairs, Department of State, in *Taiwan Communiqué and Separation Of Powers*, Hearing Before the Subcommittee on Separation of Powers of the Committee on the Judiciary, United States Senate, 98th Congress, 1st Session, on the Taiwan Relations Act and the Joint Communiqué Signed by the United States And Peking, March 10, 1983, p. 9.

46. See testimony of Holdridge, p. 17.

47. See "State Department's Responses to Additional Questions Submitted for the Record," in *China and Taiwan*, p. 32.

48. See "Interview with President Reagan," in Appendix, Additional Submissions for the Record," *Taiwan Communiqué and Separation of Powers*, p. 29.

49. Ibid.

50. *Taiwan Communiqué and Separation of Powers*, p. 19.

51. "Getting Tough with China," *Washington Times*, September 8, 1992, p. C2.

52. Nicholas Kristof, "Stung by Sale of Jets to Taiwan, China Tells France to Close Office," *New York Times*, December 24, 1992, p. A1.

53. See Giovanni de Briganti, "Dutch, Germans May End Taiwan Arms Ban," *Defense News* 7, no. 48 (November 30–December 6, 1992): 1.

54. "Mirage Deal Now Official," *China Post* (International Airmail Edition), January 7, 1993, p. 1.

55. Ibid.

6

China's Threat to Taiwan

On May 1, 1991, President Lee Teng-hui of the Republic of China, proclaimed the termination of the "Period of Mobilization for the Suppression of Communist Rebellion," formally ending Taiwan's 40-year-long state of war with the People's Republic of China. Taipei has also acknowledged the Chinese Communist Party's de facto rule over mainland China, and it no longer refers to the party as a rebellious group of "bandits." Perhaps equally significant, recent years have witnessed an explosion in economic relations between the two Chinas. Bilateral trade has surged to roughly US $6 billion per year, and Taiwanese investment in the mainland has climbed to over US $9 billion.[1]

Is the cold war between Taiwan and the PRC over? Is the likelihood of conflict across the Taiwan Strait diminishing? If so, how should the US respond to these developments? This chapter assesses the PRC's security threat to Taiwan. It discusses the conditions under which the PRC might employ force to resolve the unification issue and examines those factors that may increase or decrease Beijing's threat to Taiwan.

BEIJING'S MILITARY OPTION

The PRC has attempted to resolve the Taiwan issue by force on three separate occasions: when Generalissimo Chiang Kai-shek's army retreated to the island in 1949, when fighting broke out over the offshore islands in 1954, and when fighting broke out over the offshore islands again in 1958. In each of these cases, however, US intervention proved decisive, and Taiwan survived.

In the late 1970s, Beijing modified its approach toward Taiwan. Belligerent threats of "liberation" were replaced with impassioned appeals for "unification." On September 30, 1981, Beijing offered Taiwan a nine-point unification proposal under its "one country–two systems" formula. Under this arrangement, Taiwan would be allowed to "maintain a high degree of autonomy as a special administrative region." The points also contained assurances that Taiwan would be allowed to maintain its present socioeconomic system, its own armed forces and private property rights. Furthermore, government officials would be invited to "take up post of leadership" in Beijing. The precise timing and terms of unification would be negotiated by the CCP and Taiwan's dominant political party, the Kuomintang.

Although Beijing claims that it seeks the peaceful unification of China, it has not ruled out the use of force to take Taiwan. Officials offer a number of explanations to rationalize this contradiction. President Yang Shangkun contends that "this doesn't mean we intend to attack Taiwan. . . . Our possible use of military force is aimed at foreign countries which want to take Taiwan away from China."[2] Authorities elsewhere have suggested that Beijing cannot rule out coercion because "if we promised to relinquish the use of force, these people [Taiwan] would wax brazen and never accept peace negotiations."[3]

Under what conditions might the PRC attack Taiwan? Military officials in Taiwan have identified six situations they believe Beijing might employ as pretexts for an invasion of Taiwan:

1. If and when the island declares itself "independent;"
2. If and when an internal upheaval occurs on the island;
3. If and when the ROC Armed Forces on Taiwan become comparatively weak;
4. If and when any foreign power interferes in Taiwan's internal affairs;
5. If and when we protractedly refuse to talk with them about the issue of unification, and
6. If and when we develop nuclear weapons.[4]

During the mid-1980s, Deng Xiaoping suggested that the PRC would employ force to unify the country under the following circumstances:

If Taipei leaned toward Moscow instead of Washington; if Taipei decided to build nuclear weapons; if Taipei claimed to be an independent state; if Taipei lost internal control as a result of the succession process; or if Taipei continued to reject reunification talks for a long period of time.[5]

In recent years, however, PRC officials have cited only three situations under which coercion would be applied against Taipei: if Taiwan delayed "too much" in reunification, if Taiwan sought independence from the mainland, or if the island were "invaded" by foreign forces.[6]

Delays in Reunification

It is difficult to decipher the meaning of "too much delay." To intellectuals accustomed to thinking in terms of dynasties, it might mean centuries. To others, it might mean five or ten years. And to mainland China's aging leadership, it could mean five or ten months.

From time to time, reports surface that Beijing has set a timetable for the resolution of the Taiwan issue.   In September 1990, Hong Kong newspapers reported that unification must be achieved by the mid-1990s.   Otherwise, Beijing will exercise its military option.   In August, 1991, Hong Kong's *Cheng Ming Monthly* wrote that Deng Xiaoping has ordered that unification be achieved within three years and quoted him as saying that "we can't leave the Taiwan problem unsolved indefinitely."[7]   In October 1991, the Hong Kong-based *South China Morning Post* reported that "senior cadres are saying that Deng has decided to use the military option if the KMT does not agree to begin reunification talks by the end of 1992."[8]   PRC authorities, however, have denied all such reports.

Independence

Both Beijing and Taipei maintain that there is only one China and that Taiwan is part of it.   Mainland authorities have long cited the establishment of a Taiwan republic as one of the conditions under which the PRC would feel justified in exercising its military option toward the island.   As calls for independence have grown in Taiwan, so have Beijing's threats against the Taiwanese independence movement.

"Invasion" by Foreign Forces

During the height of the Sino-Soviet split (the late 1960s and 1970s), apprehension grew in Beijing that Taiwan might enter into some sort of an alliance with the Soviet Union or otherwise attempt to play the so-called Russian card.   The present condition is probably an extension of Deng's 1985 threat to employ force if Taipei leans toward Moscow.   It refers to the stationing of any foreign troops on Taiwan's soil.

CONSIDERATIONS THAT MAY INCREASE BEIJING'S THREAT TO TAIWAN DURING THE 1990s

The PRC's military options against Taiwan range from a naval blockade of the island to full-scale invasion. Some analysts warn that several considerations increase the probability of military confrontation during the 1990s: the nature of the Beijing regime, the PRC's growing military capabilities, the rise of the Taiwan independence movement, the reduced risk to China from the Soviet Union and the prospect of succession struggles after Deng's death.

Nature of the Beijing Regime

At both the provincial and national level in China, power is wielded by an aging clique of hard-line Communist revolutionaries, some of whom hold no formal posts within the government. For many, the Chinese Civil War remains an unfinished task. They long to see the KMT crushed and Taiwan brought back into China before they die.

These individuals lend a degree of uncertainty to the future of Taiwan-mainland relations. During an interview with the author, Chang Shallyen, Taiwan's Vice Minister of Foreign Affairs, opined that "you don't know what they really think—the old guard—they might have strange ideas."[9] Dr. Shaw Yu-ming, then Director-General of Taiwan's Government Information Office, observed that "anything can happen. . . . That regime is unpredictable."[10]

The PRC'S Growing Military Capabilities

Throughout the 1980s, the PRC sought to improve its military capabilities. These efforts continue. In March 1993, Beijing announced that military spending would rise approximately 15 percent for the year.[11] This marks the PRC's fourth consecutive year of increased defense spending. The drive toward military modernization is beginning to yield some dividends. The PRC's navy, traditionally a coastal defense force, is developing a limited regional power projection capability. Moreover, the military's minelaying capabilities have been strengthened significantly. Consequently, a US government study warns that the PLA navy may constitute a growing threat to the security of Taiwan during the 1990s:

Naval modernization will constitute an increased threat to Taiwan. The threat could manifest itself through an increased emphasis on antishipping roles or a blockade of the island. It would be difficult for Taiwan to counter either of these operations effectively.[12]

Perhaps most worrisome to Taiwan was Beijing's announcement that it has negotiated the purchase of a squadron of 24 advanced Su27 combat aircraft from the Soviet Union—aircraft that are far more advanced than anything the PRC's air force previously owned. These fighters will be stationed on Hainan Island, approximately 1,300 kilometers from Taiwan. With a combat radius of 1,500 kilometers, the jets' combat capability will cover almost the entire South China Sea and the Taiwan Strait. Although this threat appears to be directed against Vietnam or any nation that might claim jurisdiction over the Spratly Islands, Taiwan's Defense Minister, Chen Li-an, has admitted candidly that the fighters are "something worth worrying about."[13] There are also reports that Beijing is negotiating the purchase of IL-76 transport planes, an aircraft carrier and refueling technology that would give its bombers a range of approximately 1,000 miles.

The PRC's military buildup may not be motivated by a desire to attack or blockade Taiwan. Irrespective of Beijing's motivations, however, the cost of defeating Taiwan may be decreasing as the PLA improves its combined forces and amphibious operations capabilities and continues its modernization programs. If the price associated with a violent resolution of the Taiwan issue becomes low enough, the PRC might be willing to pay it.

Rise of Taiwan Independence

Beijing's position toward Taiwan independence has not softened. Following Taiwan's December 1989 Legislative Yuan elections, a contest in which independence became an issue, PRC President Yang Shangkun threatened that "it is very dangerous for Taiwan to pursue independence. . . . If the phenomenon of independence appears in Taiwan, we will not just sit there and watch."[14] In June 1991, the PRC's official newspaper, the *People's Daily (Renmin Ribao)*, branded the island's independence activists as "scum" and warned of immediate action if they continue to pursue their activities.[15]

Belligerent threats escalated sharply in October 1991, after Taiwan's main opposition party, the DPP, adopted a resolution calling for an independent Republic of Taiwan. The *People's Daily* called upon the island's independence activists to cease their operations: "otherwise they will end up smashed to bits, alienated from the Chinese race . . . which will regard them as the dregs of the race, serving Western separatist forces."[16] PRC officials warned that "if they turn a deaf ear and continue with their scheme to split the nation and sell its territory, then the Chinese Government will not sit idly by and remain indifferent."[17] According to Hong Kong accounts, senior CCP officials are hinting that the PLA is making preparations for an invasion of Taiwan.[18]

Perhaps fearing that its harsh rhetoric was helping to fuel separatist sentiment, Beijing toned down its attacks on the independence movement prior to Taiwan's December 1992 Legislative Yuan elections. During the campaign, however, the PRC's official media repeatedly warned Taiwan's voters not to support the DPP and accused the opposition party of "hurting the

[Chinese] race and harming Taiwan."[19] Following the election—a contest in which the DPP enjoyed a surprisingly strong showing at the polls—an editorial in the *People's Daily* warned ominously that "advocating an independent Taiwan cannot be called patrotism . . . rather, [these are] acts that destroy the unity of the motherland."[20] A commentary in one of Hongkong's major pro-Beijing newspapers (*Ta Kung Pao*), was even more direct:

If Taiwan's political development follows the DPP's concept of "one China, one Taiwan," it would cause social turmoil, and confrontation between people of different provincial origins would become obvious and would even turn into riots. If . . . an "independence situation" appears, the 1.1 billion compatriots [in the PRC] would not stand by with folded arms.[21]

Authorities on Taiwan believe that if the chorus of voices advocating Taiwanese independence continues to grow during the 1990s, the probability of PRC military action against Taiwan may also rise. Chung Hu-ping, Director-General of the KMT's Overseas Affairs Department, predicts that "if Taiwan really goes independent, definitely the Chinese Communists will attack Taiwan."[22] The ROC's *1992 National Defense Report* lists the circumstances under which the PRC might attack Taiwan and concludes, "The most likely one under which the Chicoms [Chinese Communists] would invade is if and when Taiwan declares itself independent; and that is also the most dangerous one to Taiwan."[23] The island's residents agree. A 1991 Gallup poll found that 57 percent of respondents believe that Beijing will attack if calls for independence are realized.[24]

The End of the Cold War

During the height of the Sino-Soviet split, a substantial contingent of China's military was deployed along the Sino-Soviet border. The PLA was charged with the responsibility of tying down an estimated 46 Soviet divisions—somewhere between 750,000 and 1,000,000 troops—as well as mobile, multiple-warhead SS-20 intermediate-range ballistic missiles and supersonic Backfire bombers. The reduction of the Soviet threat will enable the PRC to free up these forces and transfer troops and weaponry to locations where they might threaten Taiwan's security. At the same time, the easing of tensions with Hanoi will enable Beijing to shift forces away from the Sino-Vietnamese border area.

The end of the Cold War could also increase Beijing's military threat in other ways. Some speculate that the PRC may seek to resolve the unification issue by force before the United States and other Western powers have time to construct an interventionist "New World Order."[25]   Others, including President Lee Teng-hui, believe that the Beijing regime has been so affected by the failure of the Soviet coup and the collapse of communism that it "may resort to all sorts of provocations in the Taiwan Strait."[26]

Finally, the collapse of the Soviet Union has encouraged independence elements in Taiwan. Citing the newly independent Baltic states and the disintegration of the Soviet Union and Yugoslavia as examples, they see a global trend toward self-determination and separatism. Some activists claim that the time has arrived for Taiwan to proclaim its *de jure* independence from China and apply for admission to the United Nations under the name "Republic of Taiwan." These calls could increase Beijing's military threat to Taiwan.

Succession Struggles after Deng's Death

Deng Xiaoping, an octogenarian, is widely assumed to be in poor health. Paul Wolfowitz, US Under Secretary of Defense for Policy, has warned that "Chinese political dynamics will remain volatile as Deng Xiaoping passes from the scene and various factions contend for control."[27] A struggle for leadership is a distinct possibility. Taiwan officials caution that "given the history of mainland China, we believe that factional struggles will be inevitable for some period of time [and] . . . they might represent a threat to Taiwan."[28]

In such an unstable atmosphere, one faction or another might find it expedient to divert the attention of China's population and/or military by engineering a crisis with Taiwan. As Shaw Yu-ming observed, "When a dictatorship is in a very desperate state of affairs, it may resort to external aggression to resolve its internal difficulties."[29]

CONSIDERATIONS THAT MAY DECREASE BEIJING'S THREAT TO TAIWAN DURING THE 1990s

Although some trends appear to increase the probability of military confrontation across the Taiwan Strait, others seem to reduce the likelihood of hostilities.

Meeting the PRC's Prerequisities for an Attack

It is doubtful that Taiwan will meet any of the prerequisites for PRC military action. Taiwanese independence, the factor most widely considered to guarantee an attack, is unlikely. Although pro-independence sentiment has grown on the island, public opinion polls consistently reveal that a vast majority of the island's populace still do not support such a move (Table 6.1).

The KMT's disappointing showing in the 1992 Legislative Yuan election should not be interpreted as a vote for separatism. More likely is the possibility that Taiwan's voters rebelled against politicians supported by Taiwan's tycoons (the so-called Golden Oxen) and corruption. Furthermore, Taiwan's military might not tolerate independence. Premier Hau Pei-tsun, formerly Taiwan's

Table 6.1
Percentage of Taiwan's Population Favoring Independence
(May 1993)

Very Much	Yes	Hard to Say	Not Very Much	Absolutely Not
5%	18.7%	9.1%	41.4%	12.9%

Source: Public Opinion Research Foundation, Republic of China, as reported in "KMT support on decline, a poll shows," *China Post* (International Airmail Edition, May 10, 1993), p. 1.

Defense Minister, has cautioned that "the ROC [Taiwan] armed forces will not defend Taiwan in the cause of independence."[30] He has also warned that "if our country's name and national flag are changed by advocates of independence, they are not worthy of our loyalty."[31]

It is also unlikely that Taiwan will meet any other preconditions for an attack. "Delays" toward unification are not increasing the PRC's military threat to Taiwan. Communist officials view the recent growth in economic and cultural exchanges as the first steps toward unification. Furthermore, the stationing of foreign bases on the island is a very remote possibility.

Continued American Support

In 1979, the Taiwan Relations Act (TRA) was passed by the US Congress and subsequently signed into law by President Jimmy Carter. The TRA basically outlines the nature of US-Taiwan relations for the US-PRC post-normalization period. According to the TRA, it is the policy of the US to "make available to Taiwan such defense articles and defense services in such quantity as may be necessary to enable Taiwan to maintain a sufficient self-defense capability." In compliance with the TRA, the US continues to transfer large quantities of arms and sophisticated defense-related technology to Taiwan. Perhaps most significant is the recent decision to sell 150 advanced F-16/A and F-16/B fighter aircraft to Taiwan (see Chapter 5).

In addition to providing for arms and technology, Section 2 of the TRA states that it is the policy of the US to consider any attempts to resolve the Taiwan issue by other than peaceful means, including boycotts and embargoes, "a threat to the peace and security of the Western Pacific and of grave concern to the United States." Public opinion polls in the United States reveal that 31 percent of the American population believe that their government ought to send troops if the PRC attempts an invasion of Taiwan.[32]   Although less than a majority, this response is similar to that given for an attack upon South Korea. Furthermore, support for intervention among America's foreign policy elite and public opinion leaders would be much higher. Professor John Copper, a noted authority on the Taiwan situation, has suggested that the nature of an American response would depend largely upon events that led up to an attack:

If an invasion were unprovoked, a US military response would be more likely. If provoked by a Taiwan declaration of independence or political instability in the island, US action would probably be somewhat less likely. If the US did intervene, it would be most effective in forcing Peking to stop its invasion before the use of military force occurred.[33]

US officials will not make a strict commitment to Taiwan's defense. When asked how the Clinton administration would respond to an invasion, US Secretary of State Warren Christopher declined to "discuss how we might respond to a hypothetical situation of this nature."[34]   Christopher stressed, however, that "it would be our policy to make sure that such an attack does not occur."[35]

ROC military officials believe that Washington would "weigh up the Chicoms [PRC's] threat toward Taiwan and the injuries it would impose on the US interests, and adopt proper measures."[36] But both sides of the Taiwan Strait agree that the prospect of American military intervention has long played a key role in deterring Communist Chinese aggression. The late Hu Yaobang claimed that "the powerful political support" of the United States is the "most important point" serving to deter the PRC from attempting to resolve the Taiwan issue by other than peaceful means.[37] Taiwan authorities concur with Hu's judgment. Chang Shallyen believes that America's "commitment to our security has never changed and this serves as a very effective deterrent."[38]

Finally, America's successful prosecution of the war with Iraq may have increased China's apprehension. Beijing was deeply disturbed by the remarkable display of advanced Western weapons, most of which are more than a match for any of China's military systems.

Taiwan's Formidable Defensive Capabilities

Taiwan's military is relatively well trained and well equipped, and it possesses high morale. With its active duty armed forces numbering over 424,000 and with more than 1 million trained reservists, the island's military poses a significant challenge to any potential invasion force (Table 6.2). Although plans call for a significant reduction in current troop strength, the nation's commitment to national defense remains strong.[39] President Lee contends that "national security is the root of all prosperity here, and if there is no security, there is nothing."[40] The Taiwanese population agrees with the President. Over 83 percent believe that the nation should continue to strengthen its defensive capabilities.[41]

The US move to sell advanced fighter aircraft and sophisticated anti-submarine helicopters to Taiwan and permit the coproduction of the Patriot missile system should strengthen the

Table 6.2
Active-Duty and Reserve ROC Military Personnel

Branch of Service	Active Duty	Reserves
Army	270,000	1,300,000
Navy (excluding marines)	38,000	35,000
Marines	39,000	35,000
Air Force	77,000	90,000

Source: Gregory R. Copley (ed.), *Defense and Foreign Affairs Handbook, 1990–1991*, (Alexandria, Virginia: International Media Corporation, 1990), pp. 211, 212.

island's defensive capabilities.   Chen Li-an, then Defense Minister, boasted that "should the Chinese Communists launch an attack against us, they will have to pay a higher price now."[42] Hau Pei-tsun, then Premier, agreed with the Defense Minister. Hau predicted that "the Bush administration's wise decision will help to maintain peace across the Taiwan Strait."[43] The recent purchase of 60 French warplanes should also improve Taiwan's military capabilities.

In addition to arms sales, the transfer of US technology required to produce sophisticated weaponry has accelerated. Taiwan has launched an impressive drive aimed at military modernization and self-sufficiency.   Dr. Shaw Yu-ming has described this buildup as "a day and night effort."[44] The overall objective of this campaign is to retain control of the Taiwan

Strait, the surrounding sea-lanes and its territorial airspace, while maintaining an ability to repulse an amphibious assault.

New domestically produced weapons include the Indigenous Defense Fighter, PFG-2 missile frigate, M48H tank and a variety of advanced surface-to-surface, air-to-air and anti-ship missiles, which the Defense Ministry has vowed to "produce in massive quantities."[45] The government has also revealed that the Chiashan Project, a multi-billion-dollar program that consists of underground shelters for fighter aircraft and submarine facilities in eastern Taiwan, was completed in late 1991. Finally, officials have warned that, although Taiwan may not possess nuclear weapons, it "absolutely" has the capability to manufacture them.[46]

Taiwan's military muscle is impressive. But the Defense Ministry has admitted that the PRC's combat capability is far superior. For example, navy Commander-in-Chief Admiral Yeh Chang-tung concedes that "the ships we have are already insufficient for the task of naval defense."[47] Beijing is superior to Taipei in submarines, 93 to 4; in frigates 37 to 10; and in coastal craft, 915 to 73.[48] Given such figures, is Taiwan's military capacity sufficient to deter an attack?

Chen Li-an believes that Taiwan is "strong enough to make the Peking government realize that they will pay a high price if they start a war."[49] General Chen Shou-shan, Vice Defense Minister, speculates that Taiwan is capable of "holding out for about one year" should Beijing attack.[50] Premier Hau Pei-tsun has reported to Taiwan's legislature that "to ensure the safety of Taiwan, Penghu, Kinmen, and Matsu, the (military) force is more than sufficient."[51] Washington shares Taipei's confidence. Pentagon officials warn that "before Deng Xiaoping decides to invade Taiwan, he should realize the invasion could fail—miserably. . . . Its not a foregone conclusion that China would win."[52]

Relations Across the Taiwan Strait

Economic, cultural and political exchanges between Taiwan and mainland China, contacts unthinkable only several years ago, have become common. These ties may be drawing the two Chinas into a more stable and harmonious relationship and decreasing the probability of conflict across the Taiwan Strait. In 1987, Taipei enacted a law enabling persons in Taiwan to travel to the mainland to visit relatives. Under this pretext, thousands of Taiwanese businessmen rushed to the mainland. Taiwanese trade and investment in the PRC has soared. In 1991, Beijing announced that Taiwan has replaced the United States and Japan as the largest investor in the mainland.

Mainland China hopes to preserve its cordial relationship with Taiwan. Economic exchanges with Taiwan provide the PRC with technology, employment, know-how and hard currency. Taiwan officials admit that the investments by Taiwan businessmen have helped to more than quadruple Beijing's foreign currency reserves and that investors are helping the mainland develop its economy.

Cultural exchanges lag far behind economic exchanges. Some Taiwan officials complain that cultural exchange programs are far fewer in number than trade activities and might be a better way to promote improved relations. Nevertheless, cultural interaction is growing.

Taiwan officials estimate that several thousand Taiwanese students are attending colleges and universities on the mainland. In 1990, the island sent approximately 300 athletes and officials to the Asian Games in Beijing, its largest contingent ever to travel to the PRC. Furthermore, since 1987, millions of Taiwan residents have traveled to the PRC. In addition to the businessmen, travelers have included tourists, legislators, educators, athletes, reporters, film-makers and, perhaps most important, ordinary people with relatives on the mainland.

For its part, Taiwan has begun to allow a small number of mainland travelers to visit the island. Approximately 1,000 people from the PRC travel to Taiwan each month. In September

1990, government officials announced that the number of visitors coming to Taiwan from the mainland had surpassed the number of outbound Taiwan travelers for the first time since travel restrictions were eased. Restrictions on those who are allowed to visit the island are being relaxed. For example, in early 1991, Taiwan's government announced that members of the CCP would be allowed to visit the island under the condition that they would refrain from spreading Communist propaganda.

Changes in political relations have accompanied other transformations. Taipei has declared an end to its state of war with the PRC. Moreover, a formal channel for government-to-government communication, albeit an indirect one, has been established. On April 28, 1991, a delegation representing Taiwan's Straits Exchange Foundation (SEF) traveled to Beijing for five days of talks with Communist authorities. The visit was fraught with symbolism; it represented the first time that a liaison group from Taiwan had traveled to Beijing to negotiate and establish communication channels with mainland China. This visit helped to pave the way for direct discussions between SEF Chairman Koo Chen-fu and his mainland counterpart, Wang Daohan, head of the PRC's Association for Relations Across the Taiwan Strait (ARATS), in April 1993. During these historic meetings the two sides negotiated agreements on document verification and registered mail and established a framework to institutionalize contacts between the SEF and ARATS.

Is the explosion in cultural and political exchanges across the Taiwan Strait reducing mainland China's security threat to Taiwan? Some Taiwanese officials contend that trade and investment does serve as a deterrent. Officials believe that "our investment in mainland China and indirect trade probably is another sort of assurance that they would have second thoughts before using force against us . . . It would hurt themselves because their economy would be affected if they used force against us."[53]

The People's Liberation Army

The Tiananmen Square Massacre had a profound impact upon mainland China's military. Elements within the PLA, especially those who had trained as professional soldiers during the late 1970s and 1980s, believe that the military should not have been called upon to settle what amounted to a factional quarrel within the CCP. Moreover, post-Tiananmen attempts to "put politics in command" within the military have met with resentment. According to US government estimates, "up to 50 percent of all PLA training time is now focused on politics and ideology."[54] Finally, frequent transfers and shake-ups and a tarnished public image have led to further demoralization.

All of these considerations have combined to reduce PLA morale, efficiency and professionalism. They have also reduced the probability that it could be relied upon to attack or otherwise harass Taiwan. As Professor June Teufel Dreyer, an authority on China's military, observed, "The leadership has real doubts about the willingness of the PLA to obey its orders."[55]

Mainland Chinese Population

News of the Taiwan miracle has been carried into the PRC by the more than one-half million "Taiwan compatriots" who have journeyed to the mainland since 1987. As reported in the *New York Times* and other periodicals, the PRC has been swept by "Taiwan fever."[56] The fever's symptoms include a fascination with the island's music, films, fashion, books, prosperity and, ultimately, politics. In the aftermath of Beijing's violent suppression of the democracy movement, the view that Taiwan's political modernization might serve as a model for Chinese political and economic development has grown substantially. Taiwan's recent elections (the most open and democratic in China's history) have reinforced this view.

The mainland regime would find it difficult to generate popular support for a military adventure directed against Taiwan. A rare public opinion poll conducted by the PRC's Social Survey Institute found that most Chinese respondents opposed taking military action against Taiwan—even to prevent the spread of pro-independence sentiment.[57] Military action would especially antagonize China's university students, many of whom admire Taiwan's successes and consider the Chinese Civil War to be an unfortunate and increasingly irrelevant historical event. It would also alienate the populations of China's coastal provinces, particularly those who reside in areas that enjoy the largest concentrations of Taiwanese investment (Fujian and Guangdong provinces). These considerations may reduce the likelihood of hostilities directed against Taiwan.

CONCLUSION

During his recent visit to Taiwan, former President Gerald R. Ford was asked how the United States might respond if the PRC attacked Taiwan. Ford replied, "That day [for an attack] is gone."[58] Howard Baker, former White House chief of staff, believes that "the likelihood of an invasion of Taiwan is very, very small, virtually impossible."[59] Yen Xiaqi, an exiled mainland Chinese pro-democracy activist, concurs with Baker's judgment. According to Yen, "The possibility of the Chinese Communists doing so [attacking Taiwan] is slim, and there is no need for Taiwan to keep frightening its people about the threat of Communism."[60]

On the other hand, Martin L. Lasater, president of the Pacific Council and Research Associate at Pennsylvania State University's Center for East Asian Studies, has warned that "Peking's threat to Taiwan in the 1990s will be somewhat higher than in the 1980s, despite greater interaction across the Taiwan Strait."[61] Some Taiwanese officials share Lasater's concern.[62]

Defense Minister Chen Li-an believes that Beijing's desire to take
Taiwan "is as strong as ever."[63]

Interesingly, these differing perceptions are shared by
Taiwan's population. In January 1993, public opinion polls
revealed that 33.4 percent of the island's residents believe that
Beijing has stepped up its threat to invade Taiwan, but 20 percent
believe that the danger of an invasion has declined.[64] Moreover,
when asked whether the threat from across the Taiwan Strait
would escalate over the next decade, 29.7 percent replied that it
would while 28.8 percent said it would not.[65]

Is the probability of military confrontation across the Taiwan
Strait increasing or decreasing? Despite some arguments to the
contrary, a conjunction of several long-term trends is combining
to decrease Beijing's threat to Taiwan. Continued American
support, Taiwan's defense buildup, the explosion in economic and
cultural linkages across the Taiwan Strait and discontent within
the PLA and the Chinese population as a whole are reducing the
likelihood of a PRC attack upon Taiwan.

Perhaps most significant is the astonishing growth in linkages
across the Taiwan Strait. Although a sudden resolution of the
unification issue is unlikely, recent economic, cultural and
political developments are drawing the two Chinese governments
toward a more stable and harmonious relationship. They have
generated a restructuring in the manner in which Taipei and
Beijing deal with each other. These developments reduce the
probability of military conflict across the Taiwan Strait.

It is not an exaggeration to say that the PRC's security threat
to Taiwan is at its lowest ebb since 1949. A word of caution,
however, is in order. Although improbable, hostilities are still
possible. Indeed, a 1991 study commissioned by Taiwan's
Government Information Office chronicled over 60 instances
between 1975 and 1991 in which high-ranking PRC officials
threatened to use force to resolve the Taiwan issue.[66] Given
such statistics, it is not surprising that Taiwan's National Defense
Ministry has concluded that "the most serious threat to our

national security at present is still the Chicom's [PRC's] use of force against Taiwan."[67]

The PRC fluctuates in its calculations about taking Taiwan; if the cost is high, Beijing may hesitate, but if the cost is low it may decide that the benefits of hostile actions will outweigh the costs. It is critical, therefore, that Taiwan continue to upgrade its armed forces and make every effort to prevent any further deterioration in the military balance across the Taiwan Strait. Current efforts aimed at military modernization and, when feasible, defense self-sufficiency must be accelerated. It is especially crucial that Taiwan replace its aging stock of F-5E and F-104 fighter aircraft, the backbone of the island's air defense, with the F-16, Mirage 2000-5, the IDF and other advanced warplanes. As President Lee Teng-hui observed, "The most efficient guarantee for the country's survival and development is to continue building the ROC's military might.[68]

Taiwan should also adhere to its policy of rapprochement with the PRC. Although Communist officials scoff at such claims, Taiwanese trade and investment in the mainland may eventually effect a peaceful transformation in the nation's economic and political systems. The "Taiwan experience" could serve as an agent for change, helping to bring much-needed reforms to mainland China.

For its part, the United States must continue to provide Taiwan with such defense articles as may be necessary to enable Taiwan to maintain a sufficient defense capability. Moreover, it must reiterate periodically its position that any attempt to resolve the Taiwan issue by other than peaceful means would be considered a threat to peace and security in the western Pacific.

Finally, Taiwan must use its extraordinary economic success as a diplomatic tool to strengthen its relations, official or otherwise, with governments around the world. Current efforts aimed at upgrading ties with Third World nations should be continued. Links with industrialized nations should also be expanded. Taiwan must employ its financial muscle to construct a reservoir of international support that may be called upon in the unlikely event of a crisis with the PRC. These measures will not eliminate mainland China's security threat to Taiwan. When combined with other developments explored in this chapter, however, they will further reduce the probability of conflict between the two Chinas. This bodes well for peace and stability across the Taiwan Strait and for the future of all China.

Notes

1. Estimates on Taiwan's trade and investment in the PRC vary. Indeed, according to some sources, Taiwan has invested between US $15 billion and US$25 billion in mainland China. For more information, see "Twixt handskake and armlock," *Economist*, May 22, 1993, p. 39.

2. "Yang Shangkun on China's Reunification," *Beijing Review*, November 26–December 2, 1990, pp. 15–16.

3. Tai Ming Cheung, "Talk Soft, Carry Stick," *Far Eastern Economic Review*, October 18, 1990, p. 37.

4. Ministry of National Defense, *1992 National Defense Report, Republic of China* (Taipei: Li Ming Cultural Enterprises, 1992), p. 55. Translated from the Chinese version by Ma Kainan, Major General, ROC Army.

5. See Guo-cang Huan, "Taiwan: A View from Beijing," *Foreign Affairs* 63, no. 5, (Summer 1985): 1068.

6. "Three Factors for Invasion of Taiwan Outlined by Peking Communist Official," *Free China Journal*, December 13, 1990, p. 1.

7. "Magazine Claims Deng Wants China Unified in 3 Years," *China Post* (International Airmail Edition), August 31, 1991, p. 1.

8. "Beijing Launches Campaign of Fear," *China Post* (International Airmail Edition), October 19, 1991, p. 4.

9. Author's interview with Chang Shallyen, Vice Minister of Foreign Affairs, Republic of China, Taipei, Taiwan, January 8, 1992.

10. Nicholas D. Kristof, "Mainland Threat Worrying Taiwan," *New York Times*, February 10, 1991, p. A9.

11. The PRC claims that its defense budget is US $7.4 billion. Military analysts, however, dispute these figures and contend that it represents less than half of actual military spending. For more information, see Nicholas D. Kristof, "China Raises Military Budget Despite Deficit," *New York Times*, March 17, 1993, p. A9.

12. See Robert J. Skebo, Gregory K.S. Man, and George H. Stevens, "Chinese Military Capabilities: Problems and Prospects," in *China's Economic Dilemmas in the 1990's: The Problems of Reforms, Modernization, and Interdependence,* Volume 2, Study Papers Submitted to the Joint Economic Committee, Congress of the United States (Washington, D.C.: US Government Printing Office, 1991), p. 672.

13. "Minister Says M'land Forces Superior," *China Post* (International Airmail Edition), October 30, 1990, p. 1

14. Willy Wo-lap Lam, "Beijing Steps Up Taiwan Attacks," *South China Morning Post,* December 22, 1989.

15. Quoted from "Peking Issues Warning on Taiwan Independence," *China Post* (International Airmail Edition), June 4, 1991, p. 1.

16. "Taiwan 'Playing with Fire': Beijing," *China Post* (International Airmail Edition), October 18, 1991, p. 1.

17. Nicholas D. Kristof, "Beijing Threatens Taipei Opposition," *New York Times*, October 16, 1991, p. A6.

18. See "Beijing Launches Campaign of Fear," *China Post* (International Airmail Edition), October 19, 1991, p. 4.

19. Benjamin Kang Kim, "Kuomintang's Election Setback Clouds Cross-strait Relations," *China Post* (International Airmail Edition), December 25, 1992, p. 4.

20. "Mainland Paper Labels Taiwan Independence as Unpatriotic," *China Post* (International Airmail Edition), December 26, 1992, p. 4.

21. Quoted from David Stamp, "Polls increase Beijing's H.K. worries," *China Post* (International Airmail Edition), December 28, 1992, p. 2.

22. Author's interview with Chung Hu-ping, Director General, Kuomintang Overseas Affairs Department, Taipei, Taiwan, Republic of China, January 7, 1992.

23. Ministry of National Defense, *1992 National Defense Report, Republic of China*, p. 55.

24. "57% Believe Beijing Would Invade Taiwan," *China Post* (International Airmail Edition), November 5, 1991, p. 4.

25. See Lincoln Kaye, "Double 10th Double-Talk," *Far Eastern Economic Review*, October 24, 1991, p. 21.

26. "President Cautions Taiwan on Impact of Soviet Scenario May Have on Peking Regime," *Free China Journal*, September 13, 1991, p. 1.

27. See Prepared Statement of Paul D. Wolfowitz, Under Secretary of Defense for Policy, Department of Defense, in *The President's Report on the US Military Presence in East Asia*, Hearings Before the Committee on Armed Services, US Senate, 101st Congress, 2d Session, April 19, 1990, p. 16.

28. Author's interview with Chang Shallyen, Vice Minister for Foreign Affairs, Republic of China, Taipei, Taiwan, Republic of China, January 8, 1992.

29. Author's interview with Dr. Shaw Yu-ming, Director-General of Republic of China Government Information Office, Taipei, Taiwan, Republic of China, February 16, 1990.

30. "Army Defends ROC Only," *The Free China Journal*, December 25, 1989, p. 2.

31. Ibid.

32. Sixty-three percent oppose sending troops.   For more information, see "Some US Public Support for Sending Troops if Taiwan Attacked: Poll," *China Post* (International Airmail Edition), April 12, 1991, p. 3.

33. John Copper, "ROC Must Stay Alert," *Free China Journal*, October 15, 1990, p. 5.

34. "US Not to Allow Peking to Invade Taiwan," *Central News Agency* (Taiwan), January 26, 1993.

35. Ibid.

36. See Ministry of National Defense, *1992 National Defense Report, Republic of China*, p. 59.

37. See *Implementation of the Taiwan Relations Act*, Hearing and Markup Before the Committee on Foreign Affairs and Its Subcommittee on Human Rights and International Organizations and on Asian and Pacific Affairs of the House of Representatives, 99th Congress, 2d Session on H. Con. Res. 233 and H. Con. Res. 334, May 7, June 25, and August 1, 1966, p. 147.

38. Author's interview with Chang Shallyen.

39. Like its counterpart across the Taiwan Strait, the ROC is attempting to build "a leaner, meaner military." Consequently, it plans to cut 30,000 troops in 1994. For more information on troop cuts, see "Defense Cuts on Horizon; Army Likely Major Target," *Free China Journal*, April 23, 1993, p. 2.

40. "Lee Reviews Troops Urging Caution," *China Post* (International Airmail Edition), January 21, 1991, p. 1.

41. See "Majority Favor Talk Between Taipei, Peking after May: Poll," *China Post* (International Airmail Edition), April 8, 1991, p. 4.

42. David Holley, "China May Skip Arms Talks Over Taiwan Jet Deal," *Los Angeles Times*, September 4, 1992, p. A3.

43. Ibid.

44. Author's interview with Dr. Shaw Yu-ming.

45. "Defense Minister Reveals Military Buildup Strategy," *China Post* (International Airmail Edition), February 12, 1991, p. 1.

46. See "ROC Capable of Producing Nuclear Arms," *China Post* (International Airmail Edition), December 12, 1988, p. 1.

47. Hsieh Shu-fen, "Overcoming Adversity on the Seas—The Navy Plans for the Future," *Sinorama* 16, no. 9 (September 1991): 85.

48. See Congress of the United States, Office of Technology Assessment, *Global Arms Trade: Commerce in Advanced Military Technology and Weapons* (Washington, D.C.: US Government Printing Office, 1991), p. 171.

49. "Chen Li-an Confident of ROC Defense Capabilities," *China Post* (International Airmail Edition), March 12, 1991, p. 4.

50. "Peking Might Be Eyeing an Invasion of Taiwan, with World's Attention Focused on Middle East," *Free China Journal*, November 19, 1990, p. 2.

51. "Hau: ROC Power Can Defend Taiwan," *Free China Journal*, October 18, 1990, p. 1.

52. Tony Emerson, Jeff Hoffman, Kari Huus and Marcus Mabry, "Would Beijing Dare Invade?" *Newsweek* (International Edition), December 23, 1991, p. 16.

53. Author's interview with Chang Shallyen.

54. See Skebo, Man, and Stevens, "Chinese Military Capabilities: Problems and Prospects," p. 666.

55. June Teufel Dreyer, "Role of the Military on the Mainland and the Threat to the ROC," Unpublished manuscript, 1990, p. 9.

56. See Nicholas D. Kristof, "In China, Disdain for Taiwan Turns to Envy," *New York Times*, May 4, 1989, p. A1.

57. See "Beijing People Oppose Action Against Taiwan," in *China Post* (International Airmail Edition), November 2, 1991, p. 1.

58. "Former President Ford Exchanges Views with Lee Teng-hui on Global Affairs," *China Post* (International Airmail Edition), June 10, 1991, p. 1.

59. "US Committed to Taiwan's Freedom: Howard Baker," *Free China Journal*, November 12, 1990, p. 2.

60. "Mainland Dissident Refers to Beijing Calls for Invasion as Empty Threat," *China Post* (International Airmail Edition), June 27, 1991, p. 1.

61. Martin L. Lasater has warned that the recent growth of the independence movement in Taiwan may be increasing Beijing's threat to Taiwan. For more information, see Martin L. Lasater, "Taiwan's Security in the 1990's," *Asian Outlook* 25, no. 6 (September–October 1990): 1.

62. See Kristof, "Mainland Threat Worrying Taiwan."

63. Peter Kien-hong Yu, "The JDW Interview: Dr. Li-an Chen, the Republic of China's Defense Minister, Says the Beijing Regime Still Wants to Take Over His Country," *Jane's Defence Weekly*, January 5, 1991, p. 32

64. See "ROC People Confident in Reform," *China Post* (International Airmail Edition), January 9, 1993, p. 4.

65. Ibid.

66. See *A Study of a Possible Communist Attack on Taiwan* (Taipei: Government Information Office, 1991), pp. 14–61.

67. See Ministry of National Defense, *1992 National Defense Report, Republic of China*, p. 49.

68. "Lee Vows to Enhance Military," *China Post* (International Airmail Edition), October 11, 1991, p. 1.

7

Policy Options

Now that the Cold War is over, many believe that it is time to chart a new direction for American foreign policy. In East Asia, many long-range issues—including the reunification of Korea, the normalization of relations with Vietnam and the enormous trade deficit with Japan—must be addressed. Washington may also need to make some decisions about its relationship with Taipei. As one US official noted, "We've got to do some hard thinking about Taiwan."[1]

US officials seek to develop foreign policy strategies that best further the country's national interests. This is often not as easy as one might imagine because decisionmakers rarely have the luxury of being able to identify and rank-order national goals and objectives clearly. Indeed, when confronted with conflicting goals and objectives, officials sometimes have to opt for policies that will produce the least harm rather than maximize net gains; one might characterize this as approximating "damage limitation." The current US position toward Taiwan's security is no different from any other foreign policy strategy in the sense that, when and

122 United States-Taiwan Security Ties

if the policy is no longer thought to be in the best interest of the US, it will be abandoned.

Is the current policy on Taiwan's defense, a policy that is ambiguous and contradictory, in the best interest of the United States? An examination of some possible alternatives available to the US may help to answer this question. As is so often the case, however, we may find that an optimal, best or happy policy does not exist and that decisionmakers may have to settle for a policy that produces the least harm to the national interest.

There is a range of options open to an administration if it wishes to change, alter, or otherwise revise America's security relationship with Taiwan. These options form a spectrum of sorts ranging from a complete termination of military support and assistance to placing Taiwan under America's security umbrella and providing it with carte blanche for weapons procurement. The discussion below focuses on three options and the possible consequences of each: termination of military support, a significant and visible increase in military support and an orderly and gradual decrease in military support.[2]

OPTION 1: TERMINATE MILITARY SUPPORT

In the aftermath of the Cold War, some have suggested that America should reduce its security commitments abroad. For example, Ted Carpenter, Director of Foreign Policy Studies at the Cato Institute, contends that most of America's security obligations in East Asia are obsolete relics of the Cold War. Rather than press for increased "burden sharing" in the region, Carpenter argues that "Washington's goal should be one of burden shedding."[3]

In order to terminate military support for Taiwan, an administration would first have to sponsor legislation amending or revoking the TRA. The choice of such a policy might be defended on the premise that no quantity of arms will ultimately and decisively prevent the PRC from invading and conquering

Taiwan, should the PRC decide to pursue such a course of action. Indeed, in 1982 during hearings before the Senate Committee on Foreign Relations, John H. Holdridge, Assistant Secretary of the Bureau of East Asian and Pacific Affairs in the Department of State, testified that "if the PRC wanted to take Taiwan by force of arms, it could do so."[4] Moreover, curtailing military support for Taiwan would probably reduce the likelihood that America might somehow "drift into a crisis" and become entangled in a resumption of the Chinese Civil War.[5]

A termination of military support for Taiwan would also benefit US interests by removing a long-standing source of friction between the US and the PRC. The PRC regards the US security commitment to Taiwan as an infringement upon its sovereignty. Furthermore, from Beijing's viewpoint, it is the American government, not the authorities on Taiwan, that stands in the way of a peaceful reunification of China. Authorities in Beijing insist that continued American military support for Taiwan creates a climate that encourages the Kuomintang's refusal to enter into reunification negotiations. A termination of American security ties with Taiwan, therefore, might help to pave the way for increased cooperation and the easing of tensions between the PRC and the US.

Although terminating America's security commitment to Taiwan might benefit the US in some ways, the exercise of this option could also produce negative consequences. For example, an isolated ROC, cut off by all pro-Western arms suppliers, might attempt something resembling a crash project to enhance its own defensive capabilities. To accomplish this goal, the ROC government might adopt severe austerity measures likely to trigger domestic unrest. In turn, government repression could increase, and an extremely unstable or even revolutionary situation might develop. The end result is speculative, but almost certainly it would not be in the best interest of the United States.

It is quite conceivable that, in order to avoid the potentially disastrous consequences described above, the ROC might attempt to develop nuclear weapons. Officials in Taipei acknowledge that the ROC has the capability to produce both atomic warheads and long-range guided missiles. Although the current leadership repeatedly asserts that Taiwan will not develop a nuclear capability, one cannot rule out the possibility that a successor regime may feel compelled by circumstances to adopt such a course. The development of nuclear weapons would provide Taipei with a deterrent against a possible PRC attack.

Under the real possibility of attack and invasion, Taiwan could threaten the devastation of some of mainland China's most populous cities. Any retaliatory response by the PRC would net them an incinerated and radioactive Taiwan for their troubles.[6]

The exercise of Taiwan's nuclear option, however, would critically alter the existing balance of power in the region and might very well bring about a PRC preemptive attack against the island's nuclear facilities (see Chapter 6). Once again, the United States would confront a potentially disastrous situation.

If the US terminates its military support for Taiwan, the latter might attempt to procure weapons from alternative sources. Indeed, over the years, the ROC had been encouraged by the US to purchase arms from other pro-Western governments. Unfortunately for the ROC, "most traditional European arms suppliers have shunned Taiwan, however, rather than risk Peking's counter-pressure."[7] During 1992 and 1993, the PRC succeeded in frustrating Taiwan in its attempts to procure weapons from Germany and the Netherlands. Despite the successful purchase of Mirage jets from France, ROC officials acknowledge that "in the future the US will still be our main arms supplier."[8] Finally, even if the ROC is able to purchase weapons from other sources, in the future it may not be able to secure the required additional or spare parts. This problem is well exemplified by Taiwan's inability to secure spare parts for the midget submarines it purchased in the 1970s.

The ROC could, of course, simply adopt a wait-and-see policy following the termination of American military support or what is sometimes referred to as a "muddle-through" approach to defense problems. In either case, Taiwan would face a situation of rapidly decreasing defensive capabilities. Such a situation might very well cause two unfortunate outcomes. First, an increasingly nervous Taiwanese population, holding few if any emotional ties to the mainland, might attempt to alter the international status of Taiwan by overthrowing the Kuomintang government, creating a Republic of Taiwan, and purchasing defensive weapons from abroad. One problem with such a scenario is that the roughly 2 million mainlanders on the island of Taiwan, along with a significant segment of the military and the Taiwanese population, would most likely put up quite a fight in any confrontation of this sort. Additionally, the PRC has consistently vowed to crush any movement toward an independent Republic of Taiwan (see Chapter 6). Indeed, it is ironic to note that the only thing that the Kuomintang and the Communists appear to agree upon is that there is only one China and that Taiwan is a part of it.

Another unfortunate consequence of an increasingly vulnerable Taiwan is that its weakened state might tempt the PRC to attack, blockade, or otherwise harass the island. The PRC fluctuates in its calculations about making life difficult for Taiwan; if the cost is high, the PRC may hesitate, but if the cost is low, the PRC may decide that the benefits of hostile actions will outweigh the costs. Any hostile actions directed toward Taiwan would increase instability in the region and undermine American interests.

Finally, an administration must realize that any decision to terminate military support for Taiwan would undermine Washington's credibility as a reliable ally. Following America's successful prosecution of the Persian Gulf War, it would prove most ironic if Washington decided to construct a new international order by abandoning one of the few governments that enthusiastically supported its efforts to contain communism during the Cold War.

OPTION NUMBER 2: INCREASE MILITARY SUPPORT

The collapse of the Soviet Union has led to the demise of the so-called China card and the strategic triangle thereby reducing China's importance to the United States and other Western governments. During an interview with the author, Fredrick Chien, Foreign Minister of the ROC, observed that "since the Tiananmen episode of 1989, the United States has undertaken a new evaluation of the mainland and, of course, the political disintegration of the USSR gives further impetus towards the reassessment of US policy toward mainland China."[9] Some officials in Taipei believe that Washington may now be willing to upgrade relations with the ROC:

> The collapse of the Soviet Union has meant the disappearance of the so-called 'China card.' The importance of mainland China in the eyes of the White House people definitely has decreased to a great extent because of the collapse of the Soviet Union--it is quite evident. In that regard, I think our ties with Washington, D.C. can be strengthened.[10]

Should the US significantly increase its military support for Taiwan?

An increased US commitment to Taiwan's security could take a number of forms. For example, some have suggested that Washington should "make clear to the PRC the US commitment to defend Taiwan if attacked."[11] Others believe that the US should provide Taiwan with almost carte blanche for procurement of US arms. Still others contend that Taipei should be included in any new multilateral treaty organization or collective security network that the US might help construct in post-Cold War East Asia.[12] If an administration chose to exercise any of these options, the TRA would still require it to consult with members of Congress.

If the US chose to increase its security ties with Taiwan, it is likely that one of America's most reliable and trustworthy friends would be assured of a sufficient military capability for years to come. The military capability of Taiwan would give any potential enemy, including the PRC, cause to calculate seriously whether an attack on the island was worth all the risks that such an attack would entail. Additionally, if Taiwan ever decided to negotiate with the PRC on the question of reunification, it would have the luxury of being able to negotiate from a position of strength.

If the US increased its military commitment to Taiwan, there would be little chance of Taiwan's developing a nuclear capability and Taiwan authorities would not feel compelled to divert funds into the development of an indigenous fighter jet or other cost-inefficient weapons-manufacturing schemes. Indeed, one might expect to witness increased economic prosperity followed by increased social stability. Furthermore, the US government would gain increased leverage over the authorities on Taiwan, and it could use this leverage to press Taiwan for greater concessions on contentious trade issues (copyright protection, agricultural tariff reductions, etc.). Such moves would be much easier to achieve in an atmosphere of social stability and prosperity. Finally, the US would demonstrate its credibility as an ally that can be depended upon in the post-Cold War world.

Increased military support for Taiwan would probably entail elevating American arms sales to Taiwan. These arms transfers, coming at a time when the overall demand for US weapons systems is declining, might help some key US corporations—including General Dynamics, Lockheed and McDonnel Douglas—make it through what is certain to be a painful transition period away from a Cold War economy.

If Washington opted to increase its military commitment to Taipei, however, it would have to be prepared for a negative reaction from Beijing. This could range from nothing more than a very vocal protest to an actual break in diplomatic relations and/or a destabilizing arms race across the Taiwan Strait. Under the current leadership of the PRC at the time, it is conceivable that Beijing might do little more than roundly criticize the US and then let the matter rest. Nevertheless, US officials would have to consider whether a significant and visible increase in American military support for Taiwan might not lead to a perilous deterioration in US-PRC relations.

It is important for the US to maintain a constructive working relationship with the PRC. Beijing's cooperation is essential for effective action on such global problems as the environment, population, health, arms control and proliferation. Furthermore, the PRC can make a meaningful contribution to global and regional stability:

China has been pursuing a number of policies that favor US interests. It has contributed to the international isolation of Iraq, made significant efforts to compel the Khmer Rouge to accept the emerging Cambodian political settlement, normalized relations with Indonesia, and put forward a significant proposal for shelving conflicting sovereignty claims to the islands of the South China Sea and promoting joint exploitations of the natural resources in the vicinity of these islands.[13]

A sudden or dramatic tilt in American security policy toward Taiwan might well lead Beijing to play a less constructive role in international politics.

OPTION NUMBER 3: REDUCE MILITARY SUPPORT

Adoption of this policy might entail an orderly and consistent reduction of US military support (gradually curtailing arms sales, technology transfers, etc.) for Taiwan. The US government would acquiesce to the PRC demand that Washington set an actual timetable for arms sales reductions and establish a definite arms sales termination date. Like the other options, such a policy would require an administration to sponsor legislation revising or revoking the TRA. What would be the consequences of such a policy?

First, an orderly and visible reduction of US military support for Taiwan would significantly reduce, although not eliminate, a long-standing source of tension between the PRC and the US. As PRC officials have called for the US to "gradually disengage itself [from Taiwan] so as to genuinely let the Chinese settle their own problems by themselves," such a policy might very well improve relations between the two nations.[14] Second, if a reduction in the American commitment was carried out in an orderly manner over a number of years, it might afford the ROC the necessary lead time required to develop its own weapons or establish long-term arms supply arrangements with other producers. Taiwan could conceivably enter into some sort of weapons purchasing arrangement with the former Soviet Union or other arms-exporting nations that are now strapped for cash. Third, an orderly reduction of military support for Taiwan might significantly reduce the possibility of the ROC adopting some of the more radical policies outlined above. For example, an orderly reduction of support would minimize the possibility of the emergence of a "state-of-siege" mentality and a crash program to develop weapons. This would also decrease the possibility of unpopular austerity programs, unrest and repression. Furthermore, it would decrease the likelihood of Taiwan's attempting to develop a nuclear capability. Finally, a gradual decline in America's defense commitment probably would not undermine American credibility as greatly as would a sudden and complete termination.

Although such a decision by the US would significantly reduce the possibility of any of the negative consequences mentioned, it definitely would not eliminate such possibilities. Indeed, if an administration adopts such a policy, it might find that it has simply postponed the negative outcomes discussed above.

CONCLUSION

Current American security strategy, as summarized by the
Department of Defense, calls for the maintenance of a strong,
constructive relationship with both mainland China and Taiwan:

—China continues to play an important role in the regional balance
of power. It is important that this role be a positive one consistent
with peace and stability. Its growing industrial and technical
capabilities, its large military establishment (with a military budget
which has recently increased), and its immense population make it
a major factor in any regional security equation. It now has
generally friendly and stable relations with its Asian neighbors. A
stable US–China relationship is an important element in the regional
equilibrium.

—Taiwan continues to be a political and economic success story.
Our sixth largest trading partner in the world, with hard currency
reserves over $80 billion, Taiwan is an essential factor in the
economic health of Asian and has played a constructive role in the
region. US unofficial relations with Taiwan have been strong and
mutually beneficial.[15]

In order to balance these interests, the US has adopted an
ambiguous and flexible policy toward Taiwan's defense. It is not
a perfect policy. Li Shenzhi and Zi Zhongyun, director and
deputy director respectively of the American Affairs Institute of
the Chinese Academy of Social Sciences, have criticized
American policy. They warn that Washington is attempting to
"straddle two boats:"

To keep the status quo is simply a way to escape reality for a
temporary ease. It is tantamount to having no policy, giving up
one's initiative and drifting with the events. By setting each of his
feet on a different boat, one has to decide at a certain point whether
to jump onto one boat or to fall into the water.[16]

Criticisms of American policy toward Taiwan's security do
have some merit. However, the current policy does hold some

advantages for the US. One benefit is that it allows for some flexibility that might otherwise be lost; options remain open. For example, the flexibility enables the US to assist in the defense of Taiwan if it chooses to do so—but a US response is not guaranteed. The policy also enables Washington to establish a linkage between US policy and the policies and actions of other states. If the PRC were to announce that it had completely ruled out the use of force in any attempt to seek a reunification with Taiwan, the US might accordingly reduce its security commitment to Taipei. If, on the other hand, the PRC adopted a more threatening position toward the island, the US might strengthen its military support for Taiwan. Finally, the current policy encourages both Beijing and Taipei to behave responsibly. As Richard M. Nixon observed in his book, *The Real War*, "Diplomacy often requires a delicate and intricate balance of ambiguity and straight talk, the unpredictable and the very predictable."[17] He compared international relations to a poker game in which some cards are left "down," a game that "should involve the least amount of guesswork on the part of the American and the greatest amount of guesswork on the part of the other side."[18] The "hole" card will deny one's opponent perfect information and knowledge, and this uncertainty will breed restraint. In the case of America's security commitment to Taiwan, the uncertainties associated with an American response to hostilities across the Taiwan Strait may lead both parties involved to act with restraint.

As is so often the case, the problem of continued American military support for the Republic of China on Taiwan presents US decisionmakers with a situation in which it is most difficult to arrive at a value-maximizing policy after a careful consideration and rank-ordering of national goals and objectives. US security interests in East Asia include (1) maintaining regional peace and security, (2) preserving political and economic access to the region, (3) fostering the growth of democracy and human rights and (4) stopping the proliferation of nuclear weapons and ballistic missile systems.[19] Each of the alternatives to the existing policy could undermine these interests. For example, a total termination of military support for Taiwan could destabilize the entire region while yielding little positive return to the United States. On the other hand, by significantly increasing its security commitment to Taipei, Washington would unnecessarily provoke the PRC and perhaps pave the way for a break in diplomatic relations or worse. For these reasons, the US continues to pursue its present policy on military support for Taiwan.

Notes

1. Jim Mann, "Taiwan to U.S.—We're Back!" *Los Angeles Times*, July 28, 1992, p. C1.

2. In order to exercise any of the options outlined in this study, President Clinton would first have to sponsor legislation revising or revoking the TRA. It is highly probable that this could be accomplished only after an intense and bitter political struggle.

3. See prepared statement of Ted G. Carpenter, Director, Foreign Policy Studies, Cato Institute, in *Funding Implications of the United States' Worldwide Presence*, Hearing Before the Task Force on Defense, Foreign Policy, and Space of the Committee on the Budget, House of Representatives, 102d Congress, 1st Session, December 5, 1991, p. 41.

4. See testimony of John H. Holdridge in *China and Taiwan*, Hearing Before the Committee on Foreign Relations, United States Senate, 97th Congress, p. 27.

5. Chinese scholars Li Shenzhi and Zi Zhongyun, director and deputy director respectively of the American Affairs Institute of the Chinese Academy of Social Sciences, argue that current policy holds the potential for the US to "drift into a crisis and once more involve itself in China's internal conflicts." See Richard C. Bush III, "The Role of the United States in Taiwan-PRC Relations," in Dennis Fred Simon and Michael Y. M. Kau (eds.), *Taiwan: Beyond the Economic Miracle* (Armonk, New York: M. E. Sharpe, 1992), p. 345.

6. A. James Gregor and Maria Hsia Chang, "Taiwan: The 'Wild Card' in US Defense Policy in the Far Pacific," in James C. Hsiung and

Winberg Chai (eds.), *Asian and US Foreign Policy* (New York: Praeger, 1981), p. 135.

7. Kim Dalchoong, "Sino-American Normalization and Taiwan's Security and Strategic Issues," *Journal of Asiatic Studies* 23, no. 1 (1980): 11.

8. See "Taipei to Diversify Weapons Purchases," *China Post* (International Airmail Edition), April 14, 1992, p. 4.

9. Author's interview with Dr. Fredrick Chien, Foreign Minister of the Republic of China, Taipei, Taiwan, Republic of China, July 14, 1992.

10. Author's interview with Chang Shallyen, Vice Minister of Foreign Affairs of the Republic of China, Taipei, Taiwan, Republic of China, January 8, 1992.

11. This idea was presented by Martin Lasater in his thought-provoking essay titled, "US-ROC-PRC Relations in an Era of Systemic Change," (paper delivered at the 4th Tamkang University—University of Illinois Conference at Tamkang University, Taipei, Taiwan, Republic of China, November 1992).

12. Officials in both Washington and Taipei have called for the creation of a regional collective security organization. However, US authorities have only expressed a willingness to discuss a regional security pact with Japan, South Korea, Australia, New Zealand and the six-member Association of Southeast Asian Nations. Other military powers in the region—including Russia, China, Vietnam and Taiwan—are not included. For more information, see "Lee Promotes 'Collective Security' in 'Prospects for Asia' Seminar," *China Post* (International Airmail Edition), November 13, 1992, p. 3 and "Old Alliances, New Asia," *New York Times*, March 19, 1993, p. A28.

13. See Robert Ross, "American China Policy and the Security of Asia," in National Bureau of Asian and Soviet Research, *NBR Analysis* 1, no. 3 (December 1990): p. 31.

14. See Bush, "Role of the United States in Taiwan-PRC Relations," p. 345.

15. See Department of Defense, *A Strategic Framework for the Asian Pacific Rim: Report to the Congress* (Washington, D.C.: Department of Defense, July, 1992), pp.11–12. A copy of this report was provided to the author courtesy of the House Committee on Foreign Affairs.

16. Quoted from Bush, "Role of the United States in Taiwan-ROC Relations," p. 345.

17. Richard Nixon, *The Real War* (New York: Warner Books, 1980), p. 274.

18. Ibid., p. 275.

19. See Department of Defense, *A Strategic Framework Asian Pacific Rim,* p. 13.

8

United States-Taiwan Security Ties and the End of the Cold War

Since the late 1940s, US relations with Taiwan have been steered primarily by Cold War calculations. In an effort to contain what was perceived as a global Communist conspiracy, the US supported Taiwan throughout most of the 1950s and 1960s. During this stage in Sino-American relations, Washington concluded a firm alliance with Taipei and adopted the unrealistic position that the Communist Chinese regime in Beijing did not exist.

During the 1970s, Washington attempted to enlist Beijing's strategic cooperation against Soviet expansionism. In order to accomplish this task, America downgraded relations with Taipei—a move that Senator Paul Simon (Democrat–Illinois) has criticized as "going from one extreme in China policy to another."[1]

Since the normalization of relations with Beijing, US policy toward the security of Taiwan has changed in both nuance and direction. But these changes are not as radical or extreme as some may suggest. Indeed, the US has sought to respond creatively to the constraints on military support for Taiwan imposed by the normalization of relations with the PRC, the abrogation of the 1954 Mutual Defense Treaty and the issuance of the 1982 US-PRC Joint Communiqué.

Unlike the 1954 US-ROC Mutual Defense Treaty, the Taiwan Relations Act does not specifically guarantee a US response to an attack directed against Taiwan, but neither does it rule one out. The lingering possibility of an American response helps to deter the PRC from exercising its military option and allows Taiwan to decide its own future at its own pace.

American arms sales to Taiwan continue. Between 1982 and 1991 the US sold over US \$5 billion in arms to Taiwan.[2] Moreover, America's liberal interpretation of the 1982 US-PRC Joint Communiqué, a document that seemed to pledge Washington to reduce gradually its military support for Taiwan, has enabled Washington to sell advanced weapons to Taiwan. Recent sales have included missiles, advanced fighter aircraft, and sophisticated anti-submarine helicopters.

The US has also launched a vigorous program to transfer to Taiwan the technology necessary for producing weapons. These technology transfers are helping Taiwan gradually replace its obsolete weapons systems with new ones: an advanced fighter aircraft; a second generation of warships with anti-ship, anti-air and anti-submarine capabilities; advanced versions of surface-to-surface, surface-to-air, air-to-air and anti-ship missiles; and a new main battle tank.

Lord Salisbury, the noted British statesman, once complained that the most frequent mistake in politics is clinging to the carcasses of dead policies. Salisbury's observation applies with special force to several elements of American policy toward Taiwan. With the disintegration of the Soviet Union and the end of the Cold War—changes in the international system that cannot be overstated—the time has arrived for the Washington to make some adjustments in its relations with Taipei.

Following the lead of France and other members of the European Community, the US should lift the ban on visits by cabinet level officials to Taiwan. Washington should also permit Taipei to change the name of its representative offices in the United States from the cryptic "Coordination Council for North American Affairs"—a name that gives no clue as to the identity of country that it represents—to something more befitting the status of America's sixth-largest trading partner.[3] Furthermore, the US ought to support Taiwan in its drive to play an international role commensurate with its economic importance. Taiwan's financial muscle merits its active participation in the International Monetary Fund, the World Bank, the General Agreement on Tariffs and Trade and all other major international economic organizations. Finally, the US should explore various methods by which Taiwan might be allowed to return to United Nations—if only as an observer.

It is unlikely that these adjustments in policy will jeopardize America's ties with Beijing. However, these small gestures could yield big dividends for the US. They might help US firms land a large share of the contracts available under Taiwan's gigantic US $300 billion Six-Year National Development plan. Described by *Forbes Magazine* as "the world's largest market for major construction projects," about US $100 billion of the work will be open to foreign bidding.[4]

In sum, there are several steps that Washington might take in its relations with Taiwan. These modifications, however, should not include a change in American security policy. Despite the end of the Cold War, the dilemma that has confronted American decisionmakers since the late 1960s—the desire to help Taiwan maintain an adequate self-defensive capability while simultaneously maintaining a constructive relationship with the PRC—will continue. Unlike the adjustments in policy described above, any change in America's current security commitment to Taiwan may very well prove disruptive to the dynamics of the US-PRC-Taiwan triangle. Therefore, the US should maintain its existing security relationship with Taiwan. It is likely that the current policy—albeit ambiguous and contradictory—will continue to serve American interests in a post-Cold War environment.

Notes

1. See Senator Paul Simon, "Proposal to Revitalize US Policy in Asia," *Congressional Record*, May 20, 1991, p. S6124.

2. See Defense Security Assistance Agency, *Foreign Military Sales, Foreign Ministry Construction Sales and Military Assistance Facts As of September 30, 1991* (Washington, D.C.: Data Management Division, Comptroller, DSAA, 1991).

3. It is noteworthy that Japan and numerous other governments have allowed Taiwan to upgrade the name of its representative offices.

4. Caspar W. Weinberger, "Taiwan's Rosy Future," *Forbes*, October 28, 1991, p. 33.

Appendix 1

Taiwan Relations Act
(1979)

To help maintain peace, security, and stability in the Western Pacific and to promote the foreign policy of the United States by authorizing the continuation of commercial, cultural, and other relations between the people of the United States and the people on Taiwan, and for other purposes.

Be it enacted by the Senate and House of Representatives of the United States of America in Congress assembled,

SHORT TITLE

SECTION 1. This Act may be cited as the "Taiwan Relations Act."

FINDINGS AND DECLARATION OF POLICY

SEC. 2.(a) The President having terminated governmental relations between the United States and the governing authorities on Taiwan recognized by the United States as the Republic of China prior to January 1, 1979, the Congress finds that the enactment of this Act is necessary—

(1)   to help maintain peace, security, and stability in the Western Pacific; and

(2)   to promote the foreign policy of the United States by authorizing the continuation of commercial, cultural, and other relations between the people of the United States and the people on Taiwan.

(b) It is the policy of the United States—

(1)   to preserve and promote extensive, close and friendly commercial, cultural, and other relations between the people of the United States and the people on Taiwan, as well as the people on the China mainland and all other peoples of the Western Pacific area;

(2)   to declare that peace and stability in the area are in the political, security, and economic interests of the United States, and are matters of international concern;

(3)   to make clear that the United States' decision to establish diplomatic relations with the People's Republic of China rests upon the expectation that the future of Taiwan will be determined by peaceful means;

(4)   to consider any effort to determine the future of Taiwan by other than peaceful means, including by boycotts or embargoes, a threat to the peace and security of the Western Pacific area and of grave concern to the United States;

(5)   to provide Taiwan with arms of a defensive character; and

(6)   to maintain the capacity of the United States to resist any resort to force or other forms of coercion that would jeopardize the security, or

the social or economic system, of the people on Taiwan.

(c) Nothing contained in this Act shall contravene the interest of the United States in human rights, especially with respect to the human rights of all the approximately eighteen million inhabitants of Taiwan. The preservation and enhancement of the human rights of all the people on Taiwan are hereby reaffirmed as objectives of the United States.

IMPLEMENTATION OF UNITED STATES POLICY WITH REGARD TO TAIWAN

Sec. 3. (a) In furtherance of the policy set forth in section 2 of this Act, the United States will make available to Taiwan such defense articles and defense services in such quantity as may be necessary to enable Taiwan to maintain a sufficient self-defense capability.

(b) The President and the Congress shall determine the nature and quantity of such defense articles based solely upon their judgment of the needs of Taiwan, in accordance with procedures established by law. Such determination of Taiwan's defense needs shall include review by United States military authorities in connection with recommendations to the President and the Congress.

(c) The President is directed to inform the Congress promptly of any threat to the security or the social or economic system of the people on Taiwan and any danger to the interests of the United States arising therefrom. The President and the Congress shall determine, in accordance with constitutional processes, appropriate action by the United States in response to any such danger.

APPLICATION OF LAWS;
INTERNATIONAL AGREEMENTS

Sec. 4. (a) The absence of diplomatic relations shall not affect the application of the laws of the United States with respect to Taiwan, and the laws of the United States shall apply with respect to Taiwan in the manner that the laws of the United States applied with respect to Taiwan prior to January 1, 1979.

(b) The application of subsection (a) of this section shall include, but shall not be limited to, the following:

    (1)   Whenever the laws of the United States refer or relate to foreign countries, nations, states, governments, or similar entities, such terms and shall include and such laws shall apply with respect to Taiwan.

    (2)   Whenever authorized by or pursuant to the laws of the United States to conduct or carry out programs, transactions, or other relations with respect to foreign countries, nations, states, governments, or similar entities, the President or any agency of the United States Government is authorized to conduct and carry out, in accordance with section 6 of this Act, such programs, transactions, and other relations with respect to Taiwan (including, but not limited to, the performance of services for the United States through contracts with commercial entities on Taiwan), in accordance with the applicable laws of the United States.

    (3)(A)   The absence of diplomatic relations and recognition with respect to Taiwan shall not abrogate, infringe, modify, deny, or otherwise affect in any way rights or obligations (including but not limited to those involving contracts, debts, or property interest of any kind) under the laws of the United States heretofore or hereafter acquired by or with respect to Taiwan.

(B)   For all purposes under the laws of the United States, including actions in any court in the United States, recognition of the People's Republic of China shall not affect in any way the ownership of or other rights of interest in properties, tangible and intangible, and other things of value, owned or held on or prior to December 31, 1978, or thereafter acquired or earned by the governing authorities on Taiwan.

(4)   Whenever the application of the laws of the United States depends upon the law that is or was applicable on Taiwan or compliance therewith, the law applied by the people on Taiwan shall be considered the applicable law for that purpose.

(5)   Nothing in this Act, nor the facts of the President's action in extending diplomatic recognition to the People's Republic of China, the absence of diplomatic relations between the people on Taiwan and the United States, or the lack of recognition by the United States, and attendant circumstances thereto, shall be construed in any administrative or judicial proceeding as a basis for any United States Government agency, commission, or department to make a finding of fact or determination of law, under the Atomic Energy Act of 1954 and the Nuclear Non-Proliferation Act of 1978, to deny an export license application or to revoke an existing export license for nuclear exports to Taiwan.

(6)   For purposes of the Immigration and Nationality Act, Taiwan may be treated in the manner specified in the first sentence of section 202(b) of that Act.

(7)   The capacity of Taiwan to sue and be sued in courts in the United States, in accordance with the laws of the United States, shall not be abrogated, infringed, modified, denied, or otherwise affected in any way by the absence of diplomatic relations or recognition.

(8)   No requirement, whether expressed or implied, under the laws of the United States with respect to maintenance of diplomatic relations or recognition shall be applicable with respect to Taiwan.

(9)   Nothing in this Act may be construed as a basis for supporting the exclusion or expulsion of Taiwan from continued membership in any international financial institution or any other international organization.

OVERSEAS PRIVATE INVESTMENT CORPORATION

SEC. 5. (a) During the three-year period beginning on the date of enactment of this Act, the $1,000 per capita income restriction in clause (2) of the second undesignated paragraph of section 231 of the Foreign Assistance Act of 1961 shall not restrict the activities of the Overseas Private Investment Corporation in determining whether to provide any insurance, reinsurance, loans, or guaranties with respect to investment projects on Taiwan.

(b) Except as provided in subsection (a) of this section, in issuing insurance, reinsurance, loans, or guaranties with respect to investment project on Taiwan, the Overseas Private Insurance Corporation shall apply the same criteria as those applicable in other parts of the world.

THE AMERICAN INSTITUTE OF TAIWAN

SEC. 6. (a) Programs, transactions, and other relations conducted or carried out by the President or any agency of the United States Government with respect to Taiwan shall, in the manner and to the extent directed by the President, be conducted and carried out by or through—

    (1) The American Institute in Taiwan, a nonprofit corporation incorporated under the laws of the District of Columbia, or

    (2) such comparable successor nongovernmental entity as the President may designate (hereafter in the Act referred to as the "Institute").

(b) Whenever the President or any agency of the United States Government is authorized or required by or pursuant to the laws of the United States to enter into, perform, enforce, or have in force an agreement or transaction relative to Taiwan, such agreement or transaction shall be entered into, performed, enforced, in the manner and to the extent directed by the President, by or through the Institute.

(c) To the extent that any law, rule, regulation, or ordinance of the District of Columbia, or of any State or political subdivision thereof in which the Institute is incorporated or doing business, impedes or otherwise interferes with the performance of the functions of the Institute pursuant to this Act, such law, rule, regulation, or ordinance shall be deemed to be preempted by this Act.

SERVICES BY THE INSTITUTE TO UNITED STATES CITIZENS ON TAIWAN

SEC. 7.(a) The Institute may authorize any of its employees on Taiwan—

    (1) to administer to or take from any person an oath, affirmation, affidavit, or deposition, and to

perform any notarial which any notary public is required or authorized by law to perform within the United States;

(2)   To act as provisional conservator of the personal estates of deceased United States citizens; and

(3)   to assist and protect the interests of United States persons by performing other acts such as are authorized to be performed outside the United States for consular purposes by such laws of the United States as the President may specify.

(b) Acts performed by authorized employees of the Institute under this section shall be valid, and of like force and effect within the United States, as if performed by any other person authorized under the laws of the United States to perform such acts.

TAX EXEMPT STATUS OF THE INSTITUTE

SEC. 8.(a) This Institute, its property, and its income are exempt from all taxation now or hereafter imposed by the United States (except to the extent that section 11(a)(3) of this Act requires the imposition of taxes imposed under chapter 21 of the Internal Revenue Code of 1954, relating to the Federal Insurance Contributions Act) or by any State or local taxing authority of the United States.

(b) For purposes of the Internal Revenue Code of 1954, the Institute shall be treated as a organization described in sections 170(b)(1)(A), 170(c), 2055(a), 2106(a)(2)(A), 2522 (a), and 2522(b).

FURNISHING PROPERTY AND SERVICES TO AND OBTAINING SERVICES FROM THE INSTITUTE

SEC. 9. (a) Any agency of the United States Government is authorized to sell, loan, or lease property (including interests therein) to, and to perform administrative and technical support functions and services for the operations of, the Institute upon such terms and conditions as the President may direct. Reimbursements to agencies under this subsection shall be credited to the current applicable appropriation of the agency concerned.

(b) Any agency of the United States Government is authorized to acquire and accept services from the Institute upon such terms and conditions as the President may direct. Whenever the President determines it to be in furtherance of the purposes of this Act, the procurement of services by such agencies from the Institute may be effected without regard to such laws of the United States normally applicable to the acquisition of services by such agencies as the President may specify by Executive order.

(c) Any agency of the United States Government making funds available to the Institute in accordance with this Act shall make arrangements with the Institute for the Comptroller General of the United States to have access to the books and records of the Institute and the opportunity to audit the operations of the Institute.

TAIWAN INSTRUMENTALITY

SEC. 10. (a) Whenever the President or any agency of the United States Government is authorized or required by or pursuant to the laws of the United States to render or provide to or to receive or accept from Taiwan, any performance, communication, assurance, undertaking, or other action, such action shall, in the manner and to the extent directed by the President, be rendered or provided.

(b) The President is requested to extend to the instrumentality established by Taiwan the same number of offices and complement of personnel as were previously operated in the United States by the governing authorities on Taiwan recognized as the Republic of China prior to January 1, 1979.

(c) Upon granting by Taiwan of comparable privileges and immunities with respect to the Institute and its appropriate personnel, the President is authorized to extend with respect to the Taiwan instrumentality and its appropriate personnel, such privileges and immunities (subject to appropriate conditions and obligations) as may be necessary for the effective performance of their functions.

SEPARATION OF GOVERNMENT PERSONNEL FOR EMPLOYMENT WITH THE INSTITUTE

SEC. 11. (a)(1) Under such terms and conditions as the President may direct, any agency of the United States Government may separate from the Government service for a specified period any officer or employee of that agency who accepts employment with the Institute.

(2)   An officer or employee separated by an agency under paragraph (1) of this subsection for employment with the Institute shall be entitled upon termination of such employment to reemployment or reinstatement with such agency (or a successor agency) in an appropriate position with the attendant rights, privileges, and benefits which the officer or employee would have had or acquired had he or she not been so separated, subject to such time period and other conditions as the President may prescribe.

(3)   An officer or employee entitled to reemployment or reinstatement rights under paragraph (2) of this subsection shall, while continuously

employed by the Institute with no break in continuity of service, continue to participate in any benefit program in which such officer or employee was participating prior to employment by the Institute, including programs for compensation for job-related death, injury, or illness; programs for health and life insurance; programs for annual, sick, and other leave; and programs for retirement under any system established by the laws of the United States; except that employment with the Institute shall be the basis for participation in such programs only to the extent that employee deductions and employer contributions, as required, in payment for such participation for the period of employment with the Institute, are currently deposited in the program's or system's fund or depository. Death or retirement of any such officer or employee during approved service with the Institute prior to reemployment or reinstatement shall be considered a death in or retirement from Government service for purposes of any employee or survivor benefits acquired by reason of service with an agency of the United States Government.

(4) Any officer or employee of an agency of the United States Government who entered into service with the Institute on approved leave of absence without pay prior to the enactment of this Act shall receive the benefits of this section for the period of such service.

(b) Any agency of the United States Government employing alien personnel on Taiwan may transfer such personnel, with accrued allowances, benefits, and rights, to the Institute without a break in service for purposes of retirement and other benefits, including continued participation in any system established by the laws of the United States for the retirement of employees in which the alien was participating prior to the transfer to the Institute, except that employment with the Institute shall be creditable for retirement purposes only to the extent that employee deductions and employer contributions, as required, in payment for such participation for the period of employment with the Institute, are currently deposited in the system's fund or depository.

(c) Employees of the Institute shall not be employees of the United States, and, in representing the Institute, shall be exempt from section 207 of title 18, United States Code.

(d) (1)   For purposes of sections 911 and 913 of the Internal Revenue Code of 1954, amounts paid by the Institute to its employees shall not be treated as earned income. Amounts received by employees of the Institute shall not be included in gross income, and shall be exempt from taxation, to the extent that they are equivalent to amounts received by civilian officers and employees of the Government of the United States as allowances and benefits which are exempt from taxation under section 912 of such Code.

(2)   Except to the extent required by subsection (a)(3) of this section, service performed in the employ of the Institute shall not constitute employment for purposes of chapter 21 of such Code and title II of the Social Security Act.

REPORTING REQUIREMENT

SEC. 12. (a)   The Secretary of State shall transmit to the Congress the text of any agreement to which the Institute is party. However, any such agreement the immediate public disclosure of which would, in the opinion of the President, be prejudicial to the national security of the United States shall not be so transmitted to the Congress but shall be transmitted to the Committee on Foreign Relations of the Senate and the Committee on Foreign Affairs of the House of Representatives under an appropriate injunction of secrecy to be removed only upon due notice from the President.

(b) For purposes of subsection (a), the term "agreement" includes—

(1)   any agreement entered into between the Institute and the governing authorities on Taiwan or the instrumentality established by Taiwan; and

(2)   any agreement entered into between the Institute and an agency of the United States Government.

(c) Agreements and transactions made or to be made by or through the Institute shall be subject to the same congressional notification, review, and approval requirements and procedures as if such agreements and transactions were made by or through the agency of the United States Government on behalf of which the Institute is acting.

(d) During the two-year period beginning on the effective date of this Act, the Secretary of State shall transmit to the Speaker of the House of Representatives and the Committee on Foreign Relations of the Senate, every six months, a report describing and reviewing economic relations between the United States and Taiwan, noting any interference with normal commercial relations.

RULES AND REGULATIONS

SEC. 13. The President is authorized to prescribe such rules and regulations as he may deem appropriate to carry out the purposes of this Act. During the three-year period beginning on the effective date of this Act, such rules and regulations shall be transmitted promptly to the Speaker of the House of Representatives and to the Committee on Foreign Relations of the

Senate. Such action shall not, however, relieve the Institute of
the responsibilities placed upon it by this Act.

CONGRESSIONAL OVERSIGHT

SEC. 14. (a) The Committee on Foreign Affairs of the House
of Representatives, the Committee on Foreign Relations of the
Senate, and other appropriate committees of the Congress shall
monitor—

    (1)   the implementation of the provisions of this Act;

    (2)   the operation and procedures of the Institute;

    (3)   the legal and technical aspects of the continuing
relationship between the United States and
Taiwan; and

    (4)   the implementation of the policies of the United
States concerning security and cooperation in
East Asia.

(b) Such committees shall report, as appropriate, to their
respective Houses on the results of their monitoring.

DEFINITIONS

SEC. 15. For purposes of this act—

(1) the term "laws of the United States" includes any
statute, rule, regulation, ordinance, order, or judicial rule of
decision of the United States or any political subdivision thereof;
and

(2) the term "Taiwan" includes, as the context may
require, the islands of Taiwan and the Pescadores, the people on
those islands, corporations and other entities and associations
created or organized under the laws applied on those islands, and
the governing authorities on Taiwan recognized by the United
States as the Republic of China prior to January 1, 1979, and any

successor governing authorities (including political subdivision, agencies, and instrumentalities thereof).

AUTHORIZATION FOR APPROPRIATIONS

SEC. 16. In addition to funds otherwise available to carry out the provisions of this Act, there are authorized to be appropriated to the Secretary of State of fiscal year 1980 such funds as may be necessary to carry out such provisions. Such funds are authorized to remain available until expended.

SEVERABILITY OF PROVISIONS

SEC. 17. If any provision of this Act or the application thereof to any person or circumstance is held invalid, the remainder of the Act and the application of such provision to any other person or circumstance shall not be affected thereby.

EFFECTIVE DATE

SEC. 18. This Act shall be effective as of January 1, 1979.
Approved April 10, 1979

Appendix 2

U.S.-China Joint Communiqué (1982)

1. In the Joint Communiqué on the Establishment of Diplomatic Relations on January 1, 1979, issued by the Government of the United States of America of the People's Republic of China, the United States of America recognized the Government of the People's Republic of China as the sole legal government of China, and it acknowledged the Chinese position that there is but one China and Taiwan is part of China. Within that context, the two sides agreed that the people of the United States would continue to maintain cultural, commercial, and other unofficial relations with the people of Taiwan. On this basis relations between the United States and China between the United States were normalized.

2. The question of the United States arms sales to Taiwan was not settled in the course of negotiations between the two countries on establishing diplomatic relations. The two sides held differing positions, and the Chinese side stated that it would raise the issue again following normalization. Recognizing that this issue would seriously hamper the development of the United States–China

relations, they have held further discussions on it, during and
since the meetings between President Ronald Reagan and Premier
Zhao Ziyang and between Secretary of State Alexander M. Haig,
Jr. and Vice Premier and Foreign Minister Huang Hua in
October, 1981.

3. Respect for each other's sovereignty and territorial
integrity and non-interference in each other's internal affairs
constitute the fundamental principles guiding United States–China
relations. These principles were confirmed in the Shanghai
Communiqué of February 28, 1972, and reaffirmed in the Joint
Communiqué on the Establishment of Diplomatic Relations which
came into effect on January 1, 1979. Both sides emphatically
state that these principles continue to govern all aspects of their
relations.

4. The Chinese government reiterates that the questions of
Taiwan is China's internal affair. The Message to Compatriots
in Taiwan issued by China on January 1, 1979 promulgated a
fundamental policy of striving for peaceful reunification of the
Motherland. The Nine-Point Proposal put forward by China on
September 30, 1981 represented a further major effort under this
fundamental policy to strive for a peaceful solution to the Taiwan
question.

5. The United States Government attaches great importance
to its relations with China, and reiterates that it has no intention
of infringing on Chinese sovereignty and territorial integrity, or
interfering in China's internal affairs, or pursuing a policy of
"two Chinas" or "one China, one Taiwan." The United States
Government understands and appreciates the Chinese policy of
striving for a peaceful resolution of the Taiwan question as
indicated in China's Message to Compatriots in Taiwan issued on
January 1, 1979, and the Nine-Point Proposal put forward by
China on September 30, 1981. The new situation which has
emerged with regard to the Taiwan question also provides
favorable conditions for the settlement of the United States–China
differences over the question of United States arms sale to
Taiwan.

6. Having in mind the foregoing statements of both sides, the United States Government states that it does not seek to carry out a long-term policy of arms sales to Taiwan, that its arms sales to Taiwan will not exceed, either in qualitative or in quantitative terms, the level of those supplied in recent years since the establishment of diplomatic relations between the United States and China, and that it intends to reduce gradually its sales of arms to Taiwan, leading over a period of time to a final resolution. In so stating, the United States acknowledges China's consistent position regarding the thorough settlement of this issue.

7. In order to bring about, over a period of time, a final settlement of the question of United States arms sales to Taiwan, which is an issue rooted in history, the two governments will make every effort to adopt measures and create conditions conducive to the thorough settlement of this issue.

8. The development of United States–China relations is not only in the interests of the two peoples but also conducive to peace and stability in the world. The two sides are determined, on the principle of equality and mutual benefit, to strengthen their ties in the economic, cultural, education, scientific, technological, and other fields and make strong, joint efforts for the continued development of relations between the governments and peoples of the United States and China.

9. In order to bring about the healthy development of United States–China relations, maintain world peace, and oppose aggression and expansion, the two governments reaffirm the principles agreed on by the two sides in the Shanghai Communiqué and the Joint Communiqué on the Establishment of Diplomatic Relations. The two sides will maintain contact and hold appropriate consultations on bilateral and international issues of common interest.

Appendix 3

George Bush's Remarks to General Dynamics Employees in Fort Worth, Texas (September 2, 1992)

Thank you all very much for that welcome. And Bill Anders, thank you, Bill. It's a great pleasure to be introduced by Bill Anders, a friend of longstanding. And it's great to be back here, back home in Texas, the home of Jose Canseco. [*Laughter*] I think we're all in the wrong line of work, don't you? I'll tell you.

But let me thank Jim Mellor here. I'm glad to be back here with him. He reminded me that I flew the simulator when I was here last time. He was gracious enough, given the circumstances, not to remind me that the simulator obviously had a failure because it crashed with me at the helm there. [*Laughter*] But it was pilot error, I'm afraid. And let me also thank our two Congressmen here today, Pete Geren, Joe Barton. Mayor Granger is with us, the Mayor of Fort Worth. And look at this hardware. I guess they had General Dynamics in mind when they said, don't mess with Texas.

With all the Air Force types here, the true heroes of Desert Storm, I hate to bore you with war stories. But 48 years ago to this very day, September 2, 1944, I was shot down while on a bombing raid flying off our carrier over the island of Chichi Jima. I think if I'd only had F-16's, things might have been a lot different, a lot different. In all seriousness, I can't blame the plane I was flying. It was the best torpedo bomber ever to land on a carrier. I did learn, though, from that combat experience something that I think everybody here knows and has contributed to: Give our pilots the best, and then fight to win. Don't tie their hands behind their backs. And that's exactly what they did over there in Desert Storm.

I am very pleased to be here this afternoon, even for a brief visit. I wanted to come to General Dynamics to personally make a statement that concerns all of you, your families, and this wonderful community. I'm announcing this afternoon that I will authorize the sale to Taiwan of 150 F-16 AB aircraft, made right here in Fort Worth. We're proud to do this. This F-16 is an example of what only America and Americans can do. Only American technology, only American skill could have produced this flawless piece of craftsmanship which is sought all around the world.

Throughout this century, the marvels of American defense have saved lives, kept the peace, and defended American values. The world has seen the F-16 in action. Over the skies of Desert Storm the F-16 continued America's tradition of military excellence in more than 13,000 combat sorties. At this very moment planes like these may well be flying over Iraq to guarantee that the bully of Baghdad, Saddam Hussein, will not brutalize his own people by striking at them from the skies.

This sale of F-16's to Taiwan will help maintain peace and stability in an area of great concern to us, the Asia-Pacific region, in conformity with our law. In the last few years, after decades of confrontation, great strides have been made in reducing tensions between Taipei and Beijing. During this period, the United States has provided Taiwan with sufficient defensive capabilities to sustain the confidence it needs to reduce these tensions. That same sense of security has underpinned Taiwan's dramatic evolution toward democracy.

My decision today does not change the commitment of this administration and its predecessors to the three communiqués with the People's Republic of China. We keep our word: our one-China policy, our recognition of the P.R.C. as the sole legitimate government of China. I've always stressed that the importance of the 1982 communiqué on arms sales to Taiwan lies in its promotion of common political goals: peace and stability in the area through mutual restraint.

Your airplane, this great airplane, and this sale also sends a larger message to the American people as we consider how we're going to win the global economic competition. The weapons of defense that the world saw perform so brilliantly in Desert Storm were conceived by American research scientists, designed by American research engineers, crafted by the best workers in the world, the American working men and women. They were guided and operated by the young men and women of our volunteer Armed Forces, the very generation that will lead America into the next century.

My message is simple: No nation can defeat us when we set our minds to a task. Now we've got to turn those same energies and genius to the challenge at home, to secure our economic base, to ensure that the high-wage, high-tech jobs of the future are made in America.

The country that dropped missiles down smokestacks, that created a technological miracle like the F-16 can and will create the products the world needs in the new era of economic competition. The country that produced the most disciplined and high-skilled fighting force in history can and will find a way to utilize the talents of all of our young people. America's role as a military superpower was not preordained. It took the ingenuity of our workers, the creativity of our scientists, and the experience of our business leaders.

Now we must maintain our lead as the world's economic superpower and export superpower. And it will require the same magical combination of ingenuity and creativity and experienced leadership, the same magical combination you've created right here at General Dynamics.

Let me make one final point, one final point. Though the world is a much more peaceful place today, I will continue to fight for a strong defense budget. We cannot take a chance. We cannot take a chance.

Some are already proposing defense cuts far beyond the levels that our military experts feel are reasonable. I've had sound budget levels recommended to me by Colin Powell, by all the Joint Chiefs of Staff, by the Secretary of Defense. And now some in this political year want to slash defense budgets, slash the muscle of our defense. I do not want to see us go back to the days of the hollow Army or the return of an Air Force less strong than our needs require. And not only would some of the cuts proposed in this election year cut into the real muscle of our defense, they would needlessly throw defense workers out or work. And I will not have that.

Thank you very, very much for this welcome. And let me say it is a great pleasure to be able to support this sale. It is a great pleasure to come here and salute you, the finest workers in the world.

Thank you all. And may God bless our great country. Thank you very much. Thank you.

(**Note:** The President spoke at 5:11 p.m. at the General Dynamics facility at Carswell Air Force Base. In his remarks, he referred to William A. Anders, chief executive officer, and James R. Mellor, president, General Dynamics; and Texas Rangers baseball player Jose Canseco.)

Appendix 4

Excerpts of the Press Briefing on F-16 Sale to Taiwan, Joe Snyder, Department of State (September 3, 1992)

Q: Do you have a comment on the Chinese protest about that sale?

MR. SNYDER: Let me run down our rationale for the sale, if I could, and then I'll comment on the Chinese.

The decision to approve the sale to Taiwan of F-16 aircraft, configured for defensive purposes, followed a careful review.

The President's decision satisfies obligations under the Taiwan Relations Act to provide defense articles and services to Taiwan. It also advances the central goal of the 1982 Communiqué on arms sales to Taiwan, promoting cross-strait peace and stability.

The aging of Taiwan's air force and China's purchase of Russian Su-27 aircraft were among the factors considered in the President's decision . . .

We hope that China will take into consideration the defensive nature of these aircraft and their own recent acquisition of advanced fighter aircraft, the decline of Taiwan's air force, as F-5s and F-104s have gone out of service, and the President's strong commitment to the US-China relationship.

The Chinese did protest with us in a meeting. Our Ambassador met with their Vice Foreign Minister, Liu Huaqui, on September 2, and the Chinese delivered a protest regarding what, at that time, was the expected US decision to sell F-16s.

The protest paralleled the public statement which the Chinese Government released in Beijing yesterday.

Q: Joe, on the statement you made a minute ago, it says that this sale "advances the central goal of the 1982 agreement between the United States and China regarding Taiwan arms sales." But the agreement says, and I quote, "The United States Government states it does not seek to carry out a long-term policy of arms sales to Taiwan; and that its arms sale to Taiwan will not exceed either in qualitative or quantitative terms the level of those supplied in recent years, since the establishment of diplomatic relations between the United States and China, and that it intends to readily reduce its sale of arms to Taiwan."

How is that agreement in keeping with the—I mean, how is the sale in keeping with the agreement in which the United States agreed that it would not exceed the level of recent years and would gradually be reduced?

MR. SNYDER: What I would like to do is to focus on what the President, yesterday, called the importance of the communiqué on arms sales: It lies in its promotion of common political goals—peace and stability in the area through mutual restraint. Its the focus on "peace and stability" which we're dealing with here.

Q: Does having a focus on one part of an agreement permit the United States to violate another part of the agreement?

MR. SNYDER: Its not a violation of the other part of the agreement.

Q: Could you explain why it isn't?

MR. SNYDER: Because we are taking into account the decline in the quality of Taiwan's air force. We said we would be providing spare parts, and so forth. It's impossible now to provide the spare parts for the old aircraft that they have, and we're maintaining the quality of that air force in the only way that we have available now.

Q: Are you maintaining that supplying F-16s to Taiwan is somehow supplying spare parts? Is that why the plane is being supplied?

MR. SNYDER: It is maintaining the quality of the Taiwan air force in keeping with the times . . .

Q: Joe, did the Administration know when the President made this decision that China might pull out of international arms control negotiations as a result?

MR. SNYDER: Well, we're not sure China is going to do that.

Q: A senior Administration official said here yesterday that the United States was in contact with China privately to let them know that this was under consideration. So I'm curious about whether the Chinese red-flagged this for the United States and said,, "Hey, if you do this, we might pull out?" And did the President know that? Did he have that in order to make his calculation?

MR. SNYDER: I don't know the answer to that specifically. Let me make a comment, though, on that threat by the Chinese, which gets back to the original question, or that statement by the Chinese in regard to this sale.

In our efforts at non-proliferation, we draw a sharp distinction between those arms transfers which meet legitimate defense needs and contribute to the stability of a particular region and those that do not. Clearly, the Middle East is an area where all arms transfers have to be examined carefully in this light, and we would expect China to continue to participate in the President's arms transfer restraint initiative as befits its position as a leading arms exporter and Permanent Member of the Security Council.

The planned F-16 sale cannot be compared to the sort of massive destabilizing transfers which the President's initiative seeks to end. Such transfers can only add to the volatility of the Middle East as opposed to this sale which we believe helps to contribute to stability on both sides of the Taiwan Strait.

This sale, like previous sales, has given Taiwan the confidence and sense of security which has permitted the dramatic improvement in relations with the PRC which we've witnessed over the last decade.

Q: Can you take the question of whether China had been given, privately, a warning about this consequence?

MR. SNYDER: I'll see what we can do about it. I'm not so sure we're going to go into the details of our diplomatic exchanges, however.

Q: Are you sending a senior official to Beijing to explain this policy shift?

MR. SNYDER: We have informed the Chinese Government that Assistant Secretary William Clark is prepared to discuss our overall relations as well as the President's decision to authorize the sale of F-16 aircraft to Taiwan. Arrangements for a stop in China are not yet final. He will also stop briefly in Japan to discuss topics of bilateral regional, and international concern.

Q: Are you saying the Chinese have not yet indicated whether he would be welcome?

MR. SNYDER: We have informed them that he's prepared to do this, and we have not yet made final arrangements.

Q: Joe—

Q: Wait a minute. You have not yet made final arrangements or they haven't given you an answer yet?

MR. SNYDER: Again, without going into the details of our discussions, we don't have a stop in Beijing to announce. That is not set up yet.

Q: Can you explain, when you say that this advances peace and stability in that part of the world, what is the rationale? How does it advance peace and stability to provide these high-performance airplanes?

MR. SNYDER: The best thing I can do is quote what the President said yesterday. I think he addressed this quite well.

"In the last few years"—this is quoting the President—"after decades of confrontation, great strides have been made in reducing tensions between Taipei and Beijing.

"During this period, the US has provided Taiwan with sufficient defensive capabilities to sustain the confidence it needs to reduce these tensions. That same sense of security has underpinned Taiwan's dramatic evolution toward democracy.

"The decision"—the President's decision—"does not change the commitment of this Administration to the three communiqués of the People's Republic of China. We keep our word. Our one-China policy—our recognition of the People's Republic of China as the sole legitimate government of China."

And, as I said before, the importance of the '82 communiqué on arms sales to Taiwan lies in its promotion of common political goals: peace and stability in the area through mutual restraint.

Q: Could you give any more detail about this rationale of spare parts? What do you mean that they couldn't get spare parts and therefore you're selling this plane?

MR.SNYDER: Under the 1982 communiqué, one of the things that we undertook was to maintain the quality of Taiwan's air force. Taiwan has got older aircraft in its inventory. It's reached the point where it's impossible to maintain those older aircraft, and the new ones will be sold to them in line with the same goals that we pursued during this period to maintain stability.

Q: Nowhere in the communiqué does it say that if Taiwan can't get spare parts or anything like that, as far as my reading of it is concerned.

What is the authority that the State Department relies on in asserting that this is part of the communiqué?

MR. SNYDER: Don, I'm sorry, I didn't bring my copy of the communiqué here. You have yours. I'll see if I can find the specific citation in the communiqué, but we're confident that what we have done is fully in keeping with the spirit and the letter of the communiqué.

Q: Have you had a legal opinion on this? Has the State Department legal advisor said that this is in keeping with the communiqué?

MR. SNYDER: I don't really know. I'll check and see if that's necessary. I'll check and see if that's been done.

Q: Joe, is it your contention that these strategic arguments, which you've laid out, are the sole reason for this sale? Or were other considerations—domestic considerations—such as the need to preserve an assembly line and perhaps even the President's desire to be re-elected had something in the decision?

MR. SNYDER: Alan, since this is the State Department, we deal in foreign policy. I've discussed the decision in terms of its foreign policy rationale. I think I'll leave it at that.

Q: Let me rephrase the question: Is it your contention that these strategic considerations were the sole reason for the sale?

MR. SNYDER: No. No one has ever said that they were the sole reason for the sale.

Select Bibliography

Books

Bader, William B., and Bergner, Jeffrey T. *The Taiwan Relations Act: A Decade of Implementation.* Indianapolis: Hudson Institute, 1989.

Barnett, A. Doak. *US Arms Sales: The China-Taiwan Tangle.* Washington, D.C.: The Brookings Institution, 1982.

Borg, Dorothy, and Heinrichs, Waldo, eds. *Uncertain Years: Chinese-American Relations, 1947–1950.* New York: Columbia University Press, 1980.

Brzezinski, Zbigniew. *Power and Principle.* New York: Farrar, Straus and Giroux, 1983.

Bueler, William M. *US China Policy and the Problem of Taiwan.* Boulder, Colorado: Colorado Associated University Press, 1971.

Chang Jaw-ling Joanne. *United States–China Normalization: An Evaluation of Foreign Policy Decision Making*. Baltimore: University of Maryland School of Law OPRSCAS, 1986 (Copublished with Monograph Series in World Affairs, University of Denver).

Chang King-yuh. *ROC-US Relations Under the Taiwan Relations Act: Practice and Prospects*. Taipei: Institute of Internatonal Relations, National Chengchi University, 1988.

Cheng Chu-yuan. *Behind the Tiananmen Massacre: Social, Political and Economic Ferment in China*. Boulder, Colorado: Westview Press, 1990.

Cheng Hsiao-shih. *Party-Military Relations in the PRC and Taiwan*. Boulder, Colorado: Westview Press, 1990.

Chiao Chiao Hsieh. *Strategy for Survival*. London: Sherwood Press, 1985.

China in Crisis: The Role of the Military. Alexandria, Virginia: Jane's Defense Data, 1989.

Chiu Hungdah, ed. *China and the Taiwan Issue*. New York: Praeger, 1979.

Christian, Catrina. *Arms Transfers and Dependence*. New York: Taylor and Francis, 1988.

Clark, Cal. *Taiwan's Development: Implications for Contending Political Economy Paradigms*. Westport, Connecticut: Greenwood Press, 1989.

Clough, Ralph N. *Island China*. Cambridge: Harvard University Press, 1978.

Cohen, Marc J. *Taiwan at the Crossroads: Human Rights, Political Development and Social Change on the Beautiful Island*. Washington, D.C.: Asia Resource Center, 1988.

Cohen, Warren. *America's Response to China: A History of Sino-American Relations*. (3rd edition). New York: Columbia University Press, 1990.

Congressional Quarterly. *China Policy Since 1945*. Washington, D.C.: Congressional Quarterly, Inc., 1980.

Copper, John F. *A Quiet Revolution: Political Development in the Republic of China.* Lanham, Maryland: University Press of America, 1988.

——. *China Diplomacy: The Washington-Taipei-Beijing Triangle.* Boulder, Colorado: Westview Press, 1992.

——. *Taiwan: Nation-State or Province?* Boulder: Westview Press, 1990.

Defense and Foreign Affairs Handbook, 1987–88. Washington, D.C.: The Perth Corporation, 1987.

Defense and Foreign Affairs Handbook, 1990–91. Alexandria, Virginia: International Media Corporation, 1990.

Dellios, Rosita. *Modern Chinese Defense Strategy.* New York: St. Martin's Press, 1990.

Downen, Robert L. *Of Grave Concern: US-Taiwan Relations on the Threshold of the 1980's.* Washington, D.C.: Georgetown University, Center for Strategic and International Studies, 1981.

Dreyer, June Teufel. *Chinese Defense and Foreign Policy.* New York: Paragon, 1989.

——, ed. *Asian-Pacific Regional Security.* Washington, D.C.: Washington Institute Press, 1990.

Dulles, Foster Rhea. *American Policy Toward Communist China: 1949–1969.* New York: Thomas Crowell Company, 1972.

Fairbank, John King. *The United States and China.* Cambridge: Harvard University Press, 1980.

Feis, Herbert. *The China Tangle.* New York: Atheneum, 1967.

Feldman, Harvey, and Kim, Ilpyong J. *Taiwan in a Time of Transition.* New York: Paragon House, 1988.

Ford, Gerald. *A Time to Heal.* New York: Harper and Row, 1979.

Fu Jen-ken. *Taiwan and the Geopolitics of the Asian-American Dilemma.* New York: Praeger, 1992.

Garver, John W. *China's Decision for Rapprochement with the United States.* Boulder, Colorado: Westview Press, 1982.

Gates, Hill. *Chinese Working Class Lives: Getting By in Taiwan.* Ithaca: Cornell University Press, 1987.

George, Alexander L. *Presidential Decisionmaking in Foreign Policy.* Boulder, Colorado: Westview Press, 1980.

Gilbert, Stephen, ed.. *Security in Northeast Asia.* Boulder Colorado: Westview Press, 1988.

Gold, Thomas. *State and Society in the Taiwan Miracle.* Armonk, New York: M. E. Sharpe, Inc. 1986.

Golstein, Steven M. *Minidragons: Fragile Economic Miracles in the Pacific.* Boulder, Colorado: Westview, 1991.

Goodman, David, and Segal, Gerald, eds. *China at Forty: Mid-Life Crisis?* New York: Oxford University Press, 1989.

———. *China in the 1990's: Crisis Management and Beyond.* Oxford: Clarendon Press, 1991.

Goulden, Joseph C. *Korea: The Untold Story of the War.* New York: Oxford University Press, 1975.

Grasso, June M. *Truman's Two-China Policy.* Armonk, New York: M. E. Sharpe, 1987.

Grayson, Benson Lee, ed. *The American Image of China.* New York: Frederick Ungar, 1979.

Gregor, A. James. *Arming the Dragon.* Berkeley: University of Calfornia Press, 1989.

———. *The China Connection: US Policy and the People's Republic of China.* Stanford: Hoover Institution Press, 1986.

Haig, Alexander M. Jr. *Caveat: Realism, Reagan and Foreign Policy.* New York: Macmillan Publishing, 1984.

Harding, Harry. *A Fragile Relationship: The United States and China since 1972.* Washington, D.C.: The Brookings Institution, 1992.

———. *China's Foreign Relations In The 1980's.* New Haven: Yale University Press, 1984.

Harris, Stuart, and Cotton, James. *The End of the Cold War in Northeast Asia.* Boulder, Colorado: Lynne Rienner Publishers, 1991.

Hsiung, James C., and Chai, Winberg, eds. *Asia and US Foreign Policy*. New York: Praeger, 1981.

Hsu, Immanuel C. Y. *China Without Mao*. New York: Oxford University Press, 1982.

———. *The Rise of Modern China*. New York: Oxford University Press, 1975.

Institute for Contemporary Studies, ed. *US-Taiwan Relations: Economic and Strategic Dimensions*. San Francisco: ICS Press, 1985.

International Institute for Strategic Studies. *The Military Balance: 1991–1992*. London: Brassey's, 1991.

———. *Strategic Survey: 1991–1992*. London: Brassey's, 1992.

Joffe, Ellis. *The Chinese Army After Mao*. Cambridge: Harvard University Press, 1987.

Joseph, William A. *China Briefing, 1991*. Boulder, Colorado: Westview Press, 1992.

Kalicki, J. H. *The Pattern of Sino-American Crisis: Political-Military Interactions in the 1950's*. Cambridge: Cambridge University Press, 1975.

Kane, Anthony J. *China Briefing, 1990*. Boulder, Colorado: Westview, 1990.

Kim, Samuel. *China and the World: New Directions in Chinese Foreign Relations*. Boulder, Colorado: Westview Press, 1989.

Kissinger, Henry. *The White House Years*. Boston: Little, Brown and Company, 1979.

Knorr, Klause, and Verba, Sidney, eds. *The International System*. Princeton: Princeton University Press, 1961.

Koen, Ross Y. *The China Lobby in American Politics*. New York: Harper and Row, 1974.

Koenig, Louis W.; Hsiung, James C.; and Chang, King-yuh, eds. *Congress, the Presidency and the Taiwan Relations Act*. New York: Praeger, 1985.

Kosaka, Masataka, and Bearman, Sidney, eds. *Asian Security 1991–92*. Oxford: Brassey's, 1991.

Kuan Hsin-chi, and Brosseau, Maurice, eds. *China Review.* Hong Kong: Chinese University Press, 1991.

Kuan, John C. *A Review of US-ROC Relations, 1949-1978.* Taipei: Asia and World Institute, 1980.

——, ed. *Symposium on ROC-US Relations.* Taipei: Asia and World Institute, 1981.

Kusnitz, Leonard, A. *Public Opinion and Foreign Policy: America's China Policy, 1949-1979.* Westport, Connecticut: Greenwood Press, 1984.

Lambert, Mark, ed. *Jane's: All the World's Aircraft, 1991-92.* Alexandria, Virginia: Jane's Information Group. 1991.

Lasater Martin. *A Step Toward Democracy: The December 1989 Elections in Taiwan, Republic of China.* Washington, D.C.: AEI Press, 1990.

——. *Policy in Evolution: The US Role in China's Reunification.* Boulder, Colorado: Westview Press, 1988.

——. *The Security of Taiwan: Unraveling the Dilemma.* Washington, D.C.: Georgetown University, Center for Strategic and International Studies, 1982.

——. *The Taiwan Issue in Sino-American Strategic Relations.* Boulder, Colorado: Westview Press, 1984.

Lee Lai To. *The Reunification of China: PRC-Taiwan Relations in Flux.* New York: Praeger, 1991.

Lerman, Arthur J. *Taiwan's Politics: The Provincial Assemblyman's World.* Washington, D.C.: University Press of America, 1978.

Li, Victor, ed. *The Future of Taiwan: A Difference of Opinion.* Armonk, New York: M. E. Sharpe, 1980.

Liu, Alan P. L. *Phoenix and the Lame Lion.* Stanford: Hoover Institution Press, 1987.

Long, Simon. *Taiwan: China's Last Frontier.* New York: St. Martin's Press, 1991.

McLaurin, Ronald D., and Moon, Chung-in. *The United States and the Defense of the Pacific.* Boulder, Colorado: Westview Press, 1990.

Medvedev, Roy. *China and the Super Powers*. New York: Basil Blackwell, 1986.

Metraux, Daniel. *Taiwan's Political and Economic Growth in the Late Twentieth-Century*. New York: Edwin Mellen Press, Ltd. 1991.

Miller, Merle. *Plain Speaking: An Oral Biography of Harry S. Truman*. New York: Berkley Publishing Corporation, 1974.

Ministry of National Defense. *1992 National Defense Report, Republic of China*. Taipei: Li Ming Cultural Enterprise, Ltd., 1992.

Moody, Peter R. *Political Change on Taiwan: A Study of Ruling Party Adaptability*. New York: Praeger, 1992.

Mosher, Steven W. *China Misperceived: American Illusions and Chinese Reality*. New York: Harper Collins, 1990.

————, ed. *The United States and the Republic of China: Democratic Friends, Economic Partners and Strategic Allies*. New Brunswick, New Jersey: Transaction Press, 1990.

Myers, Ramon H., ed. *A Unique Relationship: The United States and the Republic of China under the Taiwan Relations Act*. Stanford: Hoover Institution Press, 1989.

————, ed. *Two Societies In Opposition: The Republic of China and the People's Republic of China After Forty Years*. Stanford: Hoover Institution Press, 1991.

Nixon, Richard M. *RN: The Memoirs of Richard Nixon*. New York: Warner Books, 1979.

————. *The Real War*. New York: Warner Books, 1980.

Noln, Janne E. *Military Industry in Taiwan and South Korea*. New York: St. Martin's Press, 1986.

Oksenberg, Michel, and Oxman, Robert B., eds. *Dragaon and Eagle—United States-China Relations: Past and Future*. New York: Basic Books, Inc. 1978.

Pollack, Jonathon. *The Sino-Soviet Rivalry and Chinese Security Debate*. R-2907-AF. Santa Monica, California: Rand Corporation, 1982.

Radvanyi, Janos, ed. *The Pacific in the 1990's: Economic and Strategic Change.* Lanham, Maryland: University Press of America, 1990.

Robinson, Thomas. *Asian Security.* Lanham, Maryland: University Press of America, 1990.

————. *Democracy and Development in East Asia: Taiwan, South Korea and the Philippines.* Lanham, Maryland: University Press, 1990.

Ryan, Mark. *Chinese Attitudes Toward Nuclear Weapons.* Armonk, New York: M. E. Sharpe, 1989.

Sanford, Dan C. *The Future Association of Taiwan with the People's Republic of China.* Berkeley: Institute of East Asian Studies, 1981.

Schaller, Michael. *The United States and China in the Twentieth Century.* Oxford: Oxford University Press, 1979.

Segal, Gerald. *Defending China.* New York: Oxford University Press, 1985.

————, ed. *Chinese Politics and Foreign Policy.* New York: Paul International for the Royal Institute of International Affairs, 1990.

Selochan, Viberto. *Armed Forces in Asia and the Pacific.* Boulder, Colorado: Westview Press, 1991.

Sharpe, Richard. *Jane's Fighting Ships, 1991–92.* Alexandria, Virginia: Jane's Information Group, 1991.

Shaw Yu-ming. *Beyond the Economic Miracle: Reflections on the Republic of China on Taiwan, Mainland China, and Sino-American Relations.* Taipei: Kwang Hwa Publishing Company, 1989.

————. *ROC-US Relations: A Decade After The "Shanghai Communiqué".* Taipei: Asia and World Institute, 1983.

Simon, Denis Fred, and Kau, Michael Y. M., eds. *Taiwan: Beyond the Economic Miracle.* Armonk, New York: M. E. Sharpe, 1992.

Stockholm International Peace Research Institute. *SIPRI Yearbook 1992: World Armaments and Disarmament*. Oxford: Oxford University Press, 1992.

Sutter, Robert G. *The China Quandary: Domestic Determinants of US China Policy 1972-1982*. Boulder, Colorado: Westview Press, 1983.

Tan Qingshan. *The Making of US China Policy: From Normalization to Post-Cold War Era*. Boulder, Colorado: Lynne Rienner, 1992.

The Republic of China on Taiwan Today: Views from Abroad. Taipei: Kwang Hwa Publishing, 1989.

Tien Hung-mao. *Mainland China, Taiwan and US Policy*. Cambridge: Oelgeschlager, Gunn and Hain Publishers, Inc., 1983.

————. *The Great Transition: Political and Social Change in the Republic of China*. Stanford: Hoover Institution Press, 1989.

Tierney, John, ed. *About Face: The China Decision and Its Consequences*. New Rochelle, New York: Arlington House, 1979.

Tow, William T., ed. *Building Sino-American Relations: An Analysis for the 1990's*. New York: Paragon House, 1991.

Wang Yu San. *Foreign Policy of the Republic of China on Taiwan: An Unorthodox Approach*. New York: Praeger, 1990.

William, Jack F., ed. *The Taiwan Issue*. New York: Praeger, 1979.

Winckler, Edwin, and Greenhalgh, Susan M. *Contending Approaches to the Political Economy of Taiwan*. Armonk, New York: M. E. Sharpe, 1988.

Wortzel, Larry M., ed. *China's Military Modernization: International Implications*. Westport, Connecticut: Greenwood Press, 1988.

Xiangze Jiang. *The United States and China*. Chicago: University of Chicago Press, 1988.

178

Articles

Auw, David. "The Growing Military Ties Between Peking and Washington." *Issues and Studies* 20, no. 7 (July 1984): 1-4.
Awanohara, Susumu. "Election Dynamics." *Far Eastern Economic Review* (August 20, 1992): 20.
Awanohara, Susumu, and Baum, Julian. "Pork Barrel Roll." *Far Eastern Economic Review* (September 17, 1992): 12-13.
Baum, Julian. "A Foot in the Door." *Far Eastern Economic Review* (September 17, 1992): 12-13.
————. "Steel Walls." *Far Eastern Economic Review* (July 9, 1992): 9-10.
Beyer, Lisa. "The Center Holds for Now." *Time* (September 3, 1990): 34-36.
"Boosting Firepower." *Asiaweek* (November 13, 1992): 28-36.
Borrus, Amy. "Peace Reigns, But Asia Is Stockpling Arms." *Business Week* (October 5, 1992): 61.
Carpenter, William M., and Gibert, Stephen P. "The Republic of China: A Strategic Appraisal for the Decade Ahead." *Issues and Studies* 27, no. 12 (December 1981): 12-32.
Chanda, Nayan. "A Technical Point: US Rejects China's Stance on Technology Transfers to Taiwan." *Far Eastern Economic Review* (August 28, 1986): 26-27.
Chang King-yuh. "Partnership in Transition: A Review of Recent Taipei-Washington Relations." *Asian Survey* 21, no. 6 (June 1981): 603-621.
Cheng, Arthur. "The IDF Close Up." *Sinorama* 16, no. 4 (April 1991): 24-29.
Cheng Chu-yuan. "Economic Development in Taiwan and Mainland China: A Comparison of Strategies and Performance." *Asian Affairs* 10, no. 1 (Spring 1983): 60-86.
Cheung Tai Ming. "Generals Under Fire." *Far Eastern Economic Review* (September 29, 1988): 40-41.

————. "Still gung-ho." *Far Eastern Economic Review* (May 18, 1989): 23.

————. "Talk Soft, carry stick." *Far Eastern Economic Review* (October 18, 1990): 37.

————. "The Balance Tilts." *Far Eastern Economic Review* (September 29, 1988): 40-41.

Chiu Hungdah. "Prospects for the Unification of China: An Analysis of the Views of the Republic of China on Taiwan." *Asian Survey* 23, no. 10 (October 1983): 1081-1094.

————. "The Future of US-Taiwan Relations." *Asian Affairs* 9, no. 1 (September-October 1981): 20-30.

Chou, David S. "The Role of the US President and Congress in American Foreign Policy-Making, with Special Reference to the Making and Implementation of the Taiwan Relations Act." *Issues and Studies* 20, no. 3 (March 1984): 41-66.

Copper, John F. "Will Peking Blockade the ROC?" *Asian Outlook* 26, no. 2 (January-February 1991): 9-11.

Dalchoong, Kim. "Sino-American Normalization and Taiwan's Security and Strategic Issues." *Journal of Asiatic Studies* 23, no. 1 (1980): 1-16.

De Brianti, Giovanni. "Dutch, Germans May End Taiwan Arms Ban." *Defense News* (November 30-December 6, 1992): 1-20.

Deng Xiaoping. "Deng Xiaoping on One Country, Two Systems." *Beijing Review* (February 3, 1986): 25-26.

————. "More on One Country, Two Systems." *Beijing Review* (April 6, 1987): 21-22.

Dreyer, June Teufel. "Role of the Military on the Mainland and the Threat to the Republic of China." Unpublished manuscript, 1991.

Emerson, J. Terry. "What Determines US Relations with China: The Taiwan Relations Act or the August 17, Communiqué with Beijing." *Asian Studies Center Backgrounder* (November 30, 1987): 1-12.

180   *Select Bibliography*

Emerson, Tony; Hoffman, Jeff; Huus, Kari; and Mabry, Marcus. "Would Beijing Dare Invade?" *Newsweek* (International Edition—Asia) (December 23, 1991): 16.

Frei, Daniel. "Introduction: The Problem of Dependence in the Security Policies of Small States." *Issues and Studies* 19, no. 3 (March 1983): 56-74.

Fulghum, David. "Chinese Coveting Offensive Triad." *Aviation Week and Space Technology* (September 21, 1992): 20-21.

Garver, John W. "Arms Sales, the Taiwan Question, and Sino-US Relations." *Orbis* 26, no. 4 (Winter 1983): 999-1035.

———. "Taiwan's Russian Option: Image and Reality." *Asian Survey* 18, no. 7, (July 1978): 751-766.

Godement, Francois. "Policy Dynamics." *Far Eastern Economic Review* (September 17, 1992): 26.

Goldstein, Carl. "A Tiger Seeking Claws." *Far Eastern Economic Review* (May 14, 1987): 24-26.

———. "An Independent Taiwan Is Not on the Cards." *Far Eastern Economic Review* (May 14, 1987): 28-30.

———. "KMT Power Grows Out of a Holstered Gun." *Far Eastern Economic Review* (May 8, 1986): 24-25.

———. "Taiwan: The Right Lashes Back." *Far Eastern Economic Review* (July 2, 1987): 15.

———. "The Military Weans Itself from Dependency on US." *Far Eastern Economic Review* (May 8, 1986): 26-29.

———. "The Winds of Change: KMT to Lift Martial Law and Allow Opposition Parties." *Far Eastern Economic Review* (October 30, 1986): 28-29.

Harrison, Selig. "Interview/Hu Yaobang: Peking Lashes Out at Washington-Taipei links." *Far Eastern Economic Review* (July 24, 1986): 26-27.

Hickey, Dennis Van Vranken. "America's Military Relations with the People's Republic of China: The Need for Reassessment" *Journal of Northeast Asian Studies* 7, no. 3 (Fall 1988): 29-33.

————. "American Technological Assistance, Technology Transfers and Taiwan's Drive for Defense Self-Sufficiency" *The Journal Of Northeast Asian Studies* 8, no.3, (Fall, 1989): 44–61.

————. "America's Two Point Policy and the Future of Taiwan" *Asian Survey* 28, no. 8, (August 1988): 881–896.

————. "US Arms Sales to Taiwan: Institutionalized Ambiguity." *Asian Survey* 26, no. 12 (December 1986): 1324–1336.

Huntington, Samuel P. "Political Development and Political Decay." *World Politics* 17, no.3 (April 1965): 386-430.

Hsieh Shu-fen. "A Day in the Life of a Destroyer Captain." *Sinorama* 16, no. 9 (September 1991): 94–97.

————. "Missile Speedboats—Accurate, Swift and Deadly." *Sinorama* 16, no. 9 (September 1991): 98–99.

————. "Overcoming Adversity on the Seas—The Navy Plans for the Future." *Sinorama* 16, no. 9 (September 1991): 82–93.

————. "Top Gun Locks Sights on a MiG." *Sinorama* 16, no. 4 (April 1991): 30–35.

————. "Who Rules the Skies over Taiwan?" *Sinorama* 16, no. 4 (April 1991): 6-23.

Huan Guo-cang. "Taiwan: A View from Beijing." *Foreign Affairs* 63, no. 5 (Summer 1985): 1064–1080.

Karniol, Robert. "Home-Made Missiles." *Far Eastern Economic Review* (July 30, 1987): 16.

————. "New Arms For Old." *Far Eastern Economic Review* (July 30, 1987): 15–17.

————. "Taiwan's Warheads." *Far Eastern Economic Review* (July 30, 1987): 18.

————. "Using the Loophole." *Far Eastern Economic Review* (July 30, 1987): 17.

Kaye, Lincoln. "Atomic Intentions." *Far Eastern Economic Review* (May 3, 1990): 9.

――――. "Double 10th double-talk." *Far Eastern Economic Review* (October 24, 1991): 20-21.

Lasater, Martin L. "Taiwan's Security in the 1990's." *Asian Outlook* 25, No. 6 (September–October 1990): 1-9.

――――. "The Dilemma of US Arms Sales to Beijing." *Asian Studies Center Backgrounder* (March 8, 1985): 1-5.

――――. "The Limits To US-China Strategic Cooperation." *Asian Studies Center Backgrounder* (April20, 1984): 1-14.

――――. "US-ROC-PRC Relations in an Era of Systemic Change." Paper presented at 4th Annual Tamkang University-University of Illinois Conference on US-ROC Relations, November 1992.

Lawrence, Susan. "Taiwan's Modest Proposal." *US News and World Report* (October 19, 1992): 48.

Lok, Joris Janssen. "US Benefits from European MLU." *Jane's Defence Weekly* (November 14, 1992): 8.

"Make or Break for GD." *Jane's Defence Weekly*n (August 29, 1992): 36-37.

Maynes, Charles. "America Without The Cold War." *Foreign Policy* 78, no. 1 (Spring 1990): 3-25.

Millman, Joel. "Taiwan's Central American links." *Jane's Defence Weekly* (November 26, 1988): 1330.

Moore, Jonathon. "Securing the Skies." *Far Eastern Economic Review* (December 22, 1988): 26.

Myers, Ramon. "The Contest Between Two Chinese States." *Asian Survey* 23, no. 4 (April 1983): 537-552.

Niou, Emerson M. S. "An Analysis of the Republic of China's Security Issues." *Issues and Studies* 28, no. 1 (January 1992): 82-95.

Nixon, Richard M. "Asia After Vietnam." *Foreign Affairs* 41, no.1 (October 1967): 111-125.

Oksenberg, Michael. "A Decade of Sino-American Relations." *Foreign Affairs* 61, no. 1, (Fall 1982): 175-195.

Proctor, Paul. "First IDF Delivered as Taiwan Spools Up for Full Production." *Aviation Week and Space Technology* (April 27, 1992): 38–44.

"Proposed F-16 Sale Draws Strong Protest." *Beijing Review* (September 14–20, 1992): 7–10.

Ross, Robert. "American China Policy and the Security of Asia." *NBR Analysis* 1, no. 3 (December 1990): 24–32.

Shaw Yu-ming. "Taiwan: A View from Taipei." *Foreign Affairs* 63, no. 5 (Summer 1985): 1050–1063.

Soong, James C. Y. "Divided China: The View from Taipei." *International Security Review* 7, no. 2 (Summer 1982): 301–314.

Starr, Barbara. "F-16 Sale Justified by 'Discrepancy.'" *Jane's Defence Weekly* (September 12, 1992): 5.

———. "MiG Buy May Lead to Chinese Copies." *Jane's Defence Weekly* (October 10, 1992): 18.

Starr, Barbara and Boatman, John. "USA reconsiders F-16 sale ban." *Jane's Defence Weekly* (August 8, 1992): 5.

Sutter, Robert. "US Arms Sales to Taiwan: Implications for American Interests." *Journal of Northeast Asian Studies* 1, no. 3 (September 1982): 27–40.

"Taiwan's Ching-kuo Fighter." *Jane's Defence Weekly* (January 7, 1989): 4.

"This Sale Is a Mirage." *Time* (July 13, 1992): 9.

"US Arms Sales to Taiwan Top 4190m." *Jane's Defence Weekly* (December 24, 1988): 1584.

Wang Chi-wu. "Military Preparedness snd Security Needs: Percpetions from the Republic of China on Taiwan." *Asian Survey* 21, no.6, (June 1981): 651–663.

Weinberger, Caspar. "Taiwan's Rosy Future." *Forbes* (October 28, 1991): 33.

Whiting, Allen S. "Assertive Nationalism in Chinese Foreign Policy." *Asian Survey* 23, no. 8 (August 1983): 913–933.

Ye Jianying. "Ye Jianying on Policy for Peaceful Reunification." *Beijing Review* (February 3, 1986): 24

Yin Ching-yao. "The Bitter Struggle Between the KMT and the CCP." *Asian Survey* 21, no. 6 (June 1981): 622–631.

Yu, Peter Kien-hong. "Strategic Importance of the Republic of China on Taiwan." *Asian Outlook* 26, no. 2 (January–February 1991): 19–23.

————. "The JDW Interview: Dr. Li-an Chen, the Republic of China's Defense Minister, Says the Beijing Regime Still Wants to Take Over his Country." *Jane's Defence Weekly* (January 5, 1991): 32.

Zhao, John Quansheng. "An Analysis Of Unification: The PRC Perspective." *Asian Survey* 23, no. 10 (October 1983): 1094–1114.

US Government Documents and Publications

Congressional Record. May 20, 1991.

Public Papers of the Presidents of the United States: Harry S. Truman, 1950. Washington, D.C.: GPO, 1965.

Public Papers of the Presidents of the United States: Jimmy Carter, 1979, Book I. Washington, D.C.: GPO, 1980.

Public Papers of the Presidents of the United States: Ronald Reagan, 1983, Book I. Washington, D.C.: GPO, 1984.

Public Papers of the Presidents of the United States: Ronald Reagan, 1983, Book II. Washington, D.C.: GPO, 1985.

Singer, Gaston J. "China Policy Today: Consensus, Consistence, Stability." *Department of State Bulletin* 87, no. 2119 (February 1987): 51.

U.S. Arms Control and Disarmament Agency. *World Military Expenditures and Arms Transfers: 1972–1982.* Washington, D.C.: GPO, 1984.

U.S. Arms Control and Disarmament Agency. *World Military Expenditures and Arms Transfers: 1990.* Washington, D.C.: GPO, 1992.

U.S. Congress. House. Task Force on Defense, Foreign Policy, and Space of the Committee On the Budget. *Funding Implications of The United States' Worldwide Presence.* Hearing, 102nd Congress, 1st Session, December 5, 1991.

U.S. Congress. House. Subcommittee on Asian and Pacific Affairs of the Committee on Foreign Affairs. *Future Importance of Taiwan and the Republic of China to US Security and Economic Interests.* Hearing, 93rd Congress, 1st Session, July 25, August 1, 1973.

U.S. Congress. House. Committee on Foreign Affairs and Its Subcommittees on Human Rights and International Organizations and on Asian and Pacific Affairs. *Implementation of the Taiwan Relations Act.* Hearing, 99th Congress, 2nd Session, May 7, June 25, and August 1, 1986.

U.S. Congress. House. Subcommittee on Asian and Pacific Affairs of the Committee on Foreign Affairs. *Political Developments in Taiwan.* Hearing, 98th Congress, 2nd Session, May 31, 1984.

U.S. Congress. House. Subcommittee on Asian and Pacific Affairs of the Committee on Foreign Affairs. *Taiwan: The Upcoming National Assembly Elections.* Hearing, 102nd Congress, 1st Session, September 24, 1991.

U.S. Congress. House. Committee on Foreign Affairs and Its Subcommittees on Asian and Pacific Affairs and on International Economic Policy and Trade. *United States-China Relations.* Hearing, 98th Congress, 2nd Session, April 3, 4, and June 5, 1984.

U.S. Congress. House. Committee on Foreign Affairs. *United States-Taiwan Relations Act.* Report No. 96-26, 96th Congress, 1st Session, March 3, 1979.

U.S. Congress. Senate. Committee on Armed Services. *The President's Report on yhe Military Presence in East Asia.* Hearing, 101st Congress, 2nd Session, April 19, 1990.

U.S. Congress. Senate. Committee on Foreign Relations. *China and Taiwan.* Hearing, 97th Congress, 2nd Session, August 17, 1982.

U.S. Congress. Senate. Committee on Foreign Relations. *The Future of Taiwan.* Hearing, 98th Congress, 1st Session, November 9, 1983.

U.S. Congress. Senate. Committee on Foreign Relations. *Trips to Taiwan, Hong Kong, Indonesia and Papua New Guinea.* Report by Senator Claiborne Pell, 102nd Congress, 2nd Session, April 1992.

U.S. Congess. Senate. Committee on Foreign Relations. *United States-China Relations: Today's Realities and Prospects for the Future.* Hearing, 98th Congress, 2nd Session, May 17, 1984.

U.S. Congress. Senate. Committee on the Judiciary. *Taiwan Communiqué and Separation Of Powers, Part One.* Report, June 1983. Washington, D.C.: GPO, 1983.

U.S. Congress. Senate. Subcommittee on Separation of Powers of the Committee on the Judiciary. *Taiwan Communiqué and Separation Of Powers, Part Two.* Hearing, 98th Congress, 1st Session, March 10, 1983.

U.S. Congress. House and Senate. Joint Economic Committee. *China's Economic Dilemmas in the 1990's: The Problems of Reforms, Modernization and Interdependence—Volumes 1 and 2.* Study Papers. Washington, D.C.: GPO, 1991.

U.S. Congress. Congressional Research Service. *Conventional Arms Transfers to the Third World, 1984-1991.* Washington, D.C.: Library of Congress, July 20, 1992.

U.S. Congress. Office of Technology Assessment. *Global Arms Trade: Commerce in Advanced Military Technology and Weapons.* Report. Washington, D.C.: GPO, 1991.

U.S. Department of Defense. *A Strategic Framework for the Asian Pacific Rim: Report to the Congress.* Washington, D.C.: Department of Defense, July, 1992.

U.S. Department of Defense. Defense Security Assistance Agency. *Foreign Military Sales, Foreign Military Construction Sales and Military Assistance Facts As of September 30, 1991.* Washington, D.C.: Data Management Division, Comptroller, DSAA, 1991.

U.S. Department of State. "Conference of President Roosevelt, Generalissimo Chiang Kai-shek and Prime Minister Churchill in North Africa." *Department of State Bulletin* 9, no.232 (December 4, 1943): 393.

U.S. Department of State. "No Sale of Advanced Aircraft to Taiwan." *Department of State Bulletin* 82, no. 2059 (February 1982): 39.

U.S. Department of State. "President's Statement, August 17, 1982." *Department of State Bulletin* 82, no.2067 (October 1982): 21.

U.S. Department of State. "Proclamation Defining Terms For Japanese Surrender." *Department of State Bulletin* 13, no.318 (July 29 1945): 137-138.

U.S. Department of State. "United States-China Joint Communique, August 17, 1982." *Department of State Bulletin* 82, no.2067 (October 1982): 20-22.

U.S. Department of State. "United States Policy Toward Formosa." *Department of State Bulletin* 22, no.550 (January 16, 1950): 79-81.

U.S. Department of State. *U.S. Department of State Foreign Relations of the United States 1950, Volume VI.* Washington D.C.: GPO, 1976.

U.S. Department of State. *U.S. Department of State Foreign Relations of the United States 1949, Volume VIII.* Washington D.C.: GPO, 1978.

U.S. Department of State. *U.S. Department of State Foreign Relations of the United States 1952-1954, Volume XIV, Part I.* Washington D.C.: GPO, 1985.

U.S. Department of State. *United States Relations with China.* Washington, D.C.: Department of State, Division of Publications, Office of Public Affairs, 1949.

Weekly Compilation of Presidential Documents: Monday, September 7, 1992. 28, no.36, Washington, D.C.: GPO, 1992.

ROC Government Documents and Publications

Council for Economic Planning and Development. *Taiwan Statistical Data Book, 1992.* Taipei: Council for Economic Planning and Development, July 1992.

Government Information Office. *A Study of a Possible Communist Attack on Taiwan.* Taipei: Government Information Office, 1991.

———. *Republic of China Yearbook, 1991-92.* Taipei: Kwang Hwa Publishing, 1991.

Ministry of Defense. *1992 National Defense Report.* Taipei: Li Ming Cultural Enterprise Corporation, 1992.

Interviews

Chien, Fredrick Foreign Minister, Republic of China. Interview by author, July 14, 1992. Tape recording, Taipei.

Chang Shallyen, Vice Minister of Foreign Affairs, Republic of China. Interview by author, January 8,1992. Tape recording, Taipei.

Chung Hu-ping, Director-General, Kuomintang Overseas Affaris Department. Interview by author, January 7, 1992. Tape recording, Taipei.

Shaw Yu-ming, Director-General, Government Information Office, Republic of China. Interview by author, February 16, 1990. Tape recording, Taipei.

Index

About the Author

DENNIS VAN VRANKEN HICKEY is a foreign policy analyst and assistant professor of political science at Southwest Missouri State University. He has lived and taught in the People's Republic of China, and his writings have appeared in publications such as *Asian Affairs*, *Orbis*, and *Pacific Review*.